Full Time Father

Full Time Father

HOW TO SUCCEED AS A STAY AT HOME DAD

Richard Hallows

EDITORS: RICHARD CRAZE, RONI JAY

WHiTe
LaDdEr
PRessS
new tricks for old dogs

Published by White Ladder Press Ltd
Great Ambrook, Near Ipplepen, Devon TQ12 5UL
01803 813343
www.whiteladderpress.com

First published in Great Britain in 2004

ISBN 0 9543914 6 2

British Library Cataloguing in Publication Data
A CIP record for this book can be obtained from the British Library.

Designed and typeset by Julie Martin Ltd
Cover design by Julie Martin Ltd
Cover photograph by Judy Hedger
Cover models: Scott Thompson and Hal Craze
Printed and bound by TJ International Ltd, Padstow, Cornwall

White Ladder Press

Great Ambrook, Near Ipplepen, Devon TQ12 5UL

01803 813343

www.whiteladderpress.com

For Alex and Maria, without whom none of this would
have been possible and I would still have to go to work every day.
I also wouldn't have had half as much fun.

Contents

Acknowledgements

As with most books, there have been several people who have helped with advice, guidance, information and their experience. In particular I would like to thank the stay at home fathers and their families who provided information and their experience for inclusion in the book including Darren, Neil, Amanda, Dylan, Samson, Karl, and Nick. I would also like to thank Roni Jay and Richard Craze at White Ladder for their enthusiasm, encouragement, and sense of humour.

Also my own family, especially my children Alex and Maria who provided all the experience to enable me to write this book (I hope it doesn't prove too much of an embarrassment in later life) and my wife Debbie, whose maternity leave gave me the time to write, and whose desire to continue her career, at least in part gave me the opportunity to be able to be a stay at home father.

I would also like to thank most of the companies I have worked for in the past, who provided the working experience that showed me there had to be something better than that. There is.

Introduction

There was a time, and it was not all that long ago, when men went to work and women stayed at home to look after the children. Times have changed. According to a survey conducted for Mothercare by YouGov in January 2004, 69% of all fathers would like to be able to give up work to look after their children on a full time basis.[1] That's a lot of fathers who want to spend their days pushing a trolley around the supermarket and changing nappies. After all, how hard can it be?

There are varying estimates of how many stay at home fathers there already are, and the truth is that nobody really knows how many have already taken this great leap into the world of full time parenthood. It is, however, clear that there is an increasing number of men who are making the decision to give up full time work to become a stay at home Dad. You just have to keep your eyes open around town and you will see a surprising number of men with pushchairs and a changing bag over their shoulder as they wonder how any man (for it will have been a man) could possibly decide that 17 steps was just what was needed to get into the doctor's surgery.

Becoming a stay at home father is not an easy decision to make. It is, even now, a departure from the accepted norm for family structure. However, more and more parents are considering this reversal of traditional roles as a possibility for their family. It is not only the father it affects. It is as big, or bigger, a decision for the mother as well.

---

1 Source: Mothercare Press Release, February 2004.

Going back to work while your man stays at home is a complete departure from what is traditionally expected of a mother. (There are those superwomen who have it all of course, but in reality they are something of a media myth, and they could not have it all without the army of nannies and other assistants that are denied us mere mortals.) It's not a decision that can be taken lightly by Mum or Dad. It changes almost everything in Dad's daily life, and it's a decision that can have just as big an impact on Mum, and the children as well.

There are some fathers who seem to have an extreme and unrealistic impression of what life as a stay at home Dad would be like. If you expect an idyllic existence where your partner leaves for work early in the morning, and the kids play quietly in their rooms while you have a long lie in, then you are going to be severely disappointed, and the life of a stay at home Dad is probably not for you. If you think that the days will be occupied by daytime television and the occasional game of football in the garden, then I suggest you think again.

That's not to say that the job of a stay at home Dad doesn't have some great perks; it can be a lot of fun, and it is immensely satisfying, but it does also involve a lot of hard work, mental strength, and dedication. For any stay at home Dad there are days when going to work with real grown ups seems an immensely preferable alternative to another day with the kids. Staying at home is not the easy option. However, being a stay at home Dad is not the hell on earth that some fathers seem to think it would be. While there are days that seem to be completely dedicated to clearing up after bodily functions, they are also the days without office politics, another round of redundancies, cancelled trains, or three hours on the motorway. If you gave them the chance, the vast majority of full time fathers wouldn't go back to their old life at work.

The benefits of being a father at home are beyond what any work environment can offer you. It gives you the chance to watch your kids grow up on a daily basis; the chance not only to be there for the birthdays and the sports days, but also to be the one who washed the sports kit and baked the birthday cake. Or in the early days, to be the one who baked the sports kit and washed the birthday cake. (From a distance the cooker and the washing machine can be easily confused.)

So, what's it really like to be a stay at home Dad? That's one of the questions this book will help to answer for you, especially as the one thing it won't be is what you expected. Being a stay at home Dad is full of surprises. The things you worry about never seem to happen, and the things you didn't worry about are the things that make every day more interesting than the one before. Some of the things you are likely to be worried about before you take on the role of a stay at home Dad quite probably include:

1   How am I going to cope with changing nappies all the time?
2   Are the kids going to spend all their time missing their mother?
3   What am I going to do all day?
4   What will family and friends think of me?
5   Am I going to have to do all the housework as well?

Just to set your mind at rest, the answers are:

1   You just do.
2   Almost certainly not.
3   Don't worry about it because not having enough to do is not going to be a problem.
4   Who cares? Anyway you can determine what they think to a large extent.
5   Quite probably, but it's not as bad as you think.

One thing that isn't a surprise is that being a full time father is nothing like the fatherhood presented in the glossy magazines where frighteningly good looking young men with perfect physiques stand smiling with their children on the ski slopes of expensive resorts in exotic locations. The role of the stay at home Dad is more about nappy sacks than six packs, and the money for the plane fare to that exotic location has just gone on a pram and car seat, while the choice of resort is now determined by whether they provide babysitting services or not, rather than the latest snow reports and the quality of the après-ski.

Despite this, more and more fathers are choosing to stay at home and look after the children.

HOW MANY STAY AT HOME FATHERS ARE THERE IN THE UK?

It is very difficult to estimate how many stay at home Dads there really are in the UK at the moment. There seem to be two main reasons for this:

1 While there are official figures for stay at home Mums, there are no official figures for the number of stay at home Dads.
2 Many stay at home fathers are involved in some kind of entrepreneurial or self-employed activity that would potentially exclude them from any analysis of the number of men who are at home looking after children. Where both partners work, it is estimated that in 36% of cases it is the father, more than any other individual who cares for the children.[2]

It is estimated that of the 3.1 million men classed as 'economically inactive', 155,000 of them cite looking after the family or home as being their reason for not working.[3]

Attitudes towards stay at home Dads are varied. Many working fathers will acknowledge that they would find it incredibly difficult to stay at home with the children, albeit often with a tone that suggests immense sympathy for the poor man who couldn't hold down a real job.

However, by being clear about why you are becoming a stay at home Dad and approaching the role in the right way, such misgivings can be minimised. In my experience, this is a short term problem, and part of the adjustment of moving from employment to being a stay at home Dad. Most men who have made this choice will honestly tell you that:

1   It is the most fulfilling thing they have ever done with their lives.

2   It is not an easy job, and they have worked harder as a stay at home Dad than they ever did in the office.

3   That the decision to become a stay at home Dad was the one that was the best for their family.

4   That they would not change their decision given the chance.

5   That there is nothing that could be more important for them to do than to be responsible for their children.

The numbers of stay at home Dads are very small relative to the number of stay at home mothers. It is very unclear how many there really are, or even how many would like to be stay at home Dads, but it is clear that there are more fathers taking the primary care role in their families than you may expect. The idea that a father might want to stay at home to look after his children while the mother goes to work has at least progressed to the point where most people are interested

---

2   Ferri, E and Smith, K (1995) Parenting in the 1990s. London Family Policy Study Centre. Referenced in 'What Good Are Dads?' (2001) fathersdirect.com.

3   Reported on www.homedad.org, 7th December 2003, based on Spring 2001 figures from the Office of National Statistics.

enough to have a sensible conversation about it rather than just ignorantly write you off as a complete waste of space.

WHY DID STAY AT HOME DADS MAKE THAT CHOICE?

There is no single reason why a perfectly normal father chooses to become a stay at home Dad, but there are some common themes that emerge when stay at home Dads are asked why they made the choice they did.

1 Financial Considerations

The single most common reason cited is the simple pragmatic consideration of financial practicality. This applies in particular when there is a significant differential between the salary of the father and the salary of their partner. When a double income household is being reduced to a single income, if the higher income is that of the mother, it may well be that there is effectively no choice but for the father to be the one who stays at home with the children.

2 The Cost of Professional Childcare

A part of the financial consideration is the cost of childcare. In most cases, the cost of two children in a day nursery will be in the order of £15,000 per annum.[4] This equates to a gross salary of something in the low 20 thousands. When faced with a choice of working full time in order to take home just a few thousand pounds a year after paying for full time professional childcare, the decision to provide full time parental care becomes a much easier one to take. The financial cost of giving up work to look after the children can be almost minimal, once the effects of childcare costs are entered into the equation. In almost all cases where the father has stayed at home, there is an underlying assumption that some form of parental childcare is preferable, if at all possible, to full time professional childcare.

3 Redundancy

Again, within the overall scope of finances, some fathers have taken on the role as a result of being made redundant. They often treat redundancy more as a fortunate event that provided the opportunity to become a stay at home father, rather than the role being an unfortunate result of being made redundant.

4 Focus on Partner's Career

Even when the pure financial considerations are not cited as the main reason, it is at times based on a wider decision to allow the mother to focus on her career. This may apply where the mother's job is more secure or has better chances of promotion, or where the father's career can be placed on hold without causing serious problems. This again reflects an underlying preference for parental care rather than professional childcare. Some stay at home Dads have been fortunate enough to be able to negotiate a career break in order to be able to look after the kids and then return to their employer, but this is definitely an exception and not the general rule.

5 Personal Preference

When financial issues are disregarded, the most common reason given for fathers becoming stay at home Dads is pure personal preference.

This book is not a commercial for being a stay at home Dad. There are good bits, and there are not so good bits. It does not involve long lunches with young mothers. Well not all the time.

I gave up full time work in July 2001 to become a stay at home father, while my partner returned to her (better paid and more secure) job after maternity leave. This book includes my own personal experi-

---

4 Based on £30 per day, full time for two children for 51 weeks a year, with 5% discount applied to the second child.

ences, as well as experience and advice from other men who have made the same decision.

The objective of the book is to provide you with three things.

1　A realistic idea of what it is like to be a stay at home Dad; the challenges that you would face, and the pitfalls that are waiting for you.

2　Enough information to enable you to make an informed decision as to whether being a stay at home Dad is something you might want to be. It is not for everyone.

3　Hints and tips to allow you to be a stay at home father without having to make all the same mistakes that some of us did.

There are also some things it is worth making clear that this book is not about.

1　It is not about being a single dad (through either divorce or bereavement).

2　It is not about being a stay at home Dad in a same sex partnership. (This, despite the fact that being a man with a pram seems to lead a portion of the general population to the conclusion that you must, by definition, be gay. How they managed to work this one out remains a mystery to me, but it's a fact.)

3　It is not a childcare handbook. It is not about how to feed, clothe, bathe, and wind a child, although as a stay at home father you will be doing all those things. It is about surviving as a stay at home father. I wish that someone had been able to give me this book before I started my childcare responsibilities. I don't think I would have made a different choice as a result of reading it, but I do believe I would have been better prepared. I did have a fairly unrealistic expectation at the time. (See comment regarding long lunches with young mothers.)

4　The final thing that this book is not about is telling you that you ought to be a stay at home father, or that your children will some-how be better off with a father at home than with a father work-ing. I have no evidence to support any hypothesis concerning the relative benefits of stay at home or working fathers. The reason most people make the decisions they do is because it is what is right for them and their family in their particular situation. That is the only way that any decision on who stays home to look after the children can be made, and no book can pretend to be able to tell you what will be best. This book is not on a mission to convert working fathers into stay at home fathers. It is about helping those who want to be a stay at home Dad to be as well prepared as they can be.

If you are thinking about being a stay at home Dad, good luck, enjoy the experience, and always wear loose fitting clothes with lots of pock-ets.

PART 1:
Leaving work

Introduction

It may sound obvious when you think about it, but one of the inevitable consequences of being a stay at home Dad is that you are no longer going to be making your way to work every day. However, considering what this means to you may well be pushed to the back of your mind as you continue to worry about what looking after children all day long is going to be like. Although it is obviously necessary to focus on what your new role as a stay at home Dad will mean, it is also important to think about what leaving your old life behind may mean to you.

As a result of leaving work it is likely that:

- Your family income will be significantly reduced.
- You will no longer have the social interaction that comes with your job, and you will leave behind the friends you have made over the years through your work.
- You will no longer have the job satisfaction or the pat on the back that comes with a job well done.
- You will no longer have the status or the perks that go with your job.
- You will lose the sense of belonging that you gained from your work.
- You will lose the boost to your self esteem that your job provided.

Giving up work to become a stay at home Dad is very different from taking a long vacation. It feels more as if you are retiring, and your potential to make a contribution has somehow suddenly disappeared. This can have even more of an impact if you have left work and decided to become a stay at home Dad through a compulsory redundancy or some event which has left you feeling that this is not a decision you have made freely.

The way in which people react to your decision, and the things you do to counteract the effects of no longer going to work every day, will go a long way to determining your success as a stay at home Dad. How you feel about what you are doing, and how you approach this new role, will also help to manage the impact that becoming a stay at home Dad can have on your self esteem.

Self Esteem

Of the many changes that becoming a stay at home Dad will bring to your life, one of the most common is an impact on how you feel about yourself. Although it may not feel as if becoming a stay at home Dad should be particularly bad for your self esteem, it is a common issue for many men who have made the choice to stay at home with the children. There seem to be three main causes of this:

1 The way in which you choose to become a stay at home Dad and then approach the role. If you start with a negative attitude towards why you are doing it, and what it means to be a stay at home Dad, this is clearly going to have an impact on how you feel about yourself.
2 Other people's opinions about why you are becoming a stay at home Dad and what the role means to them, and their perception of what it means for you.
3 The way you perform in your role as a stay at home Dad and your ongoing view of what you are doing and achieving, including whether you feel as if you are in control of your own life, or whether somehow you are being controlled by it.

The good news is that these feelings of low self esteem seem to be most prevalent for stay at home Dads when they first take on the role. They do not last forever; in fact they don't normally last very long at all.

In some ways, these initial feelings of low self esteem may be inevitable as fathers and the people around them get used to the idea of them staying at home with the kids, but by planning and preparing effectively, by managing other people's opinions of you, and by managing your role on a day to day basis, you can minimise any self esteem issues that may occur. You can soon reach the point where the value of what you do, and the skills and competencies that you bring to the role, are clear to you and to those around you, and you can start to feel good about yourself again.

The actual process of leaving work can be a key element in determining your initial self esteem. If you have resigned deliberately in order to stay at home with the children, this is a very different starting point from becoming a stay at home Dad due to compulsory redundancy, for example.

Almost every father has had days at work when staying at home and looking after the kids seems like the best possible career move. The idiot who tells the boss exactly what he wants to hear has just been promoted (again), the supplier who promised everything would be with you by last week isn't answering the telephone any more, and the signs have just gone up on your route to work to tell you that there will be severe delays for the next seven years. There are days when anything seems better than working for a living, and what could be better than being a full time father?

When it comes down to it though, not working for a living any more is a big thing to do. It could be described as the denial of millions of years of genetic programming designed to make men go out and hunt woolly mammoth, while the womenfolk, naturally, look after the kids.

Of course, there isn't much about working in the modern day office environment that can provide the thrills and spills of your average mammoth hunt (well, not any of the jobs I had anyway), and I can't help but imagine that the majority of us would become a part of the food chain should we ever encounter anything remotely resembling a 15 foot high shaggy elephant.

Under normal circumstances, the majority of fathers can expect to give up work when they retire. You may have fantasised that you would be so wealthy by the time you were 30 (or less) that you would never need to work again, but (and I am sorry to disappoint you) that tends to be the exception rather than the rule. Most fathers will work until they retire, or in some cases they will continue to work after they retire. I tell you this in order to be able to make clear that deciding to stay at home and look after the children is not an early retirement option.

At the age when most people are having children, we are in many ways defined by what we do for a living. Our job has become a definition of who we are and the contribution we make to society. If you give up work to look after the children, you change from being 'John the accountant' to being 'John the house husband'. This is not at all like being 'John the retired person who used to be an accountant', it is just plain 'John the house husband'. All the status and respect associated with the job has disappeared, and people who would have intuitively known how to react to 'John the accountant' have no idea at all about what to do or say when they are confronted by 'John the house husband'. For many people it is difficult for them to imagine why a man would want to be a stay at home Dad, what being a stay at home Dad involves, and whether this makes you a superhero or someone who doesn't do a lot.

Being 'John the accountant' immediately told people a lot about who you were. Depending on their view of accountants, it might have told them for example that:

- You have a university degree.
- You trained for and passed professional qualifications.
- You probably earn a reasonable salary.
- You probably work in an office and wear a suit to work, and
- You are a professional and respected person.

Being 'John the house husband' tells them that you know how to work the washing machine and you're probably quite adept with a vacuum cleaner. It is a big difference in first impressions, and a big change in how you have to see yourself.

Being a stay at home Dad is not an occupation that would suit every father. You are doing something that is still considered by many not to be a normal or healthy occupation for a man, because it isn't a traditional breadwinner role, and it is after all 'more natural' for the mother to look after the children. As a result, you have to be prepared to deal with the issues of being someone who is (even though you probably didn't know it) challenging people's perception of what the world should be like.

Leaving work is a major change for you and your family, perhaps on top of another major change of having recently started a family. It is surprising how overnight you can change from being a worthwhile and productive member of society, to being an unpaid servant whose only function is to respond to the whims of a small child.

In order to be a stay at home Dad you have to want to do it. Financial reasons alone are not sufficient to sustain the lifestyle happily. If you are spending all your time wishing you were doing something else, the chances are you will eventually resent your children for stopping you from doing these other things, and you may even start to resent your partner for still having the opportunity to do these other things. If you don't want to do it, then it is highly likely that you will not be very good at it.

Other People's Opinions

In my experience, about the only thing that can be guaranteed about other people's opinions is that everybody will have one on the subject of being a stay at home Dad.

The good news is that the biggest surprise is how many of these opinions are generally positive, especially in terms of initial reactions. The bad news is that everybody seems to think that the same things are funny. References to house-husbands, being a kept man, watching the television all day, and mother and baby clubs are barely amusing even the first time you hear them. After that they get pretty dull fairly quickly.

INITIAL REACTIONS

There seem to be two main categories of initial reaction to the idea of being a stay at home Dad.

1 The generic reactions to the general principle of a man being a stay at home father and providing childcare.
2 The specific reactions to you as an individual being a man who will stay at home and provide childcare.

Opinions will vary a lot. A person's opinion is norr
on their age, sex, whether they have children or no
tionship to you. There is nothing to say that their op
particularly well thought out, or even make sense,

can manage to hold a generic opinion about stay at home fathers that directly conflicts with their opinion of you as an individual being a stay at home father.

A close relative of mine was very vocal in their opinion that it was unnatural and just plain wrong for a man to be at home looking after the children, but clearly it was the best thing for me to do and would be of immense benefit to me, my partner, and the children.

Go figure.

INITIAL REACTIONS TO FATHERS CHOOSING TO BECOME STAY AT HOME DADS

Stay at home dads report a variety of initial reactions, including:

1 Questioning whether they are sure this is what they want to do.
2 Suggestions that they are the luckiest person in the world to be able to do this.
3 The suggestion that this is just a temporary aberration brought on by the stress of becoming a father, and that they will soon come to their senses and return to the workplace.
4 Utter shock and complete disbelief.
5 The assertion that childcare is woman's work.
6 Encouragement.

However, the overwhelming majority of responses tend to be expressed positively and they are occasionally tinged with envy as a result of the image of a stay at home Dad putting his feet up in front of the television every morning, while the children deliver him bacon sandwiches and fresh coffee.

The variation of opinions based on gender and parental status can be interesting.

SINGLE MEN

The opinions of single men tend to be along the lines of:

- 'You lucky devil'
- 'A kept man then eh?'
- 'All those young women at the mother and baby club will keep you busy.'
- 'I wish I could sit at home all day watching TV.'

My experience suggests that there is little point arguing with these views, or even in trying to have a sensible conversation about them, as there's little you can say to convince a man with no experience of children that you have not in fact achieved a state of nirvana where you do exactly what you feel like while your partner works to keep you in the manner to which you would like to be accustomed. Let them dream.

MEN WITH CHILDREN

Men with children tend to express a different range of opinions. These tend to include phrases such as "You must be mad" and "I couldn't do it." These are often accompanied by an involuntary shudder and a grimace. There are also the occasional polite enquiries as to whether you have become a 'new man' or have suddenly found a need to get in touch with your feminine side.

GENERATIONAL DIFFERENCES

There are also some generational opinions that will be expressed, in particular from older men who can be just completely confused by the whole concept of a man wanting to spend any significant amount of time with his children. The idea of being a stay at home Dad is not one they appear to comprehend. However, there are very few instances of the parents of stay at home Dads being unsupportive. It would seem that parental instincts are able to overcome any generational issues in most cases.

OTHER PEOPLE'S CONCERNS

The people closest to you, and particularly within your extended family, may express some serious concerns about the path you are taking. This will normally include sensible, practical concerns as to what becoming a stay at home Dad will do to your employment prospects, future career, and family finances. These concerns are to a certain extent inevitable, and reflect many of the concerns that you will already have.

The most significant thing you can do to allay these concerns and influence the opinions of family and friends is to provide a well thought out and convincing answer to them. This is one of the major reasons why having a long term plan from the outset is so important. In terms of influencing their opinion it doesn't really matter whether you stick to the plan or not, and where children are involved it is the plan that is the first thing to be forgotten, but it is important to show that you have thought through the issues involved.

QUESTIONS YOU NEED TO HAVE AN ANSWER FOR:

1   Why are you becoming a stay at home Dad rather than having more traditional family roles?

2   What are you going to do to keep your brain active?

3   What are you going to do when the kids go to school?

4   What are you going to do about your pension?

5   How are you going to explain your time as a stay at home Dad to any potential future employer?

6   What are you going to do if it doesn't work out and you can't stand being a stay at home Dad?

7   What are you going to do if your partner loses her job?

By being able to give well thought out and credibly convincing answers to these questions you can go a long way towards easing the minds of the people who care about you most.

When Dad stays at home to look after the children there are also concerns that relate to the mother who will need to return to work. Most stay at home fathers have not experienced any negative opinions regarding the mother's choice to return to work, and in many cases friends and family had assumed that she would return to her career after maternity leave. It was just that the expectation was that the children would be in full time professional childcare, rather than having Dad give up work to look after them. From the perspective of others' opinions, Mum returning to work seems to be somewhat easier than Dad staying at home.

WOMEN'S OPINIONS

Generally, women have a slightly different reaction to the idea of a man choosing to be stay at home Dad and look after the children. The experience of existing stay at home Dads suggests that you will inevitably, at some point, meet some who believe that a man is genetically, psychologically, and physically incapable of looking after children, and that they can certainly never look after children as well as the mother.

Once again, there is little to be gained from entering into a philosophical argument on this point. Even in 20 years time when you have proved them wrong, you will only be the exception that proves the rule.

For the majority of women, however, the word 'brave' tends to feature strongly in their reaction. There are two aspects to this bravery:

1 There is the bravery you are displaying by taking on the role of looking after the children in the first place. It is not an easy job.
2 Secondly, it is a brave choice because you are doing something that is not the norm, and you have got to work your way through a system and society that is completely geared towards the mother being the primary carer. In my view, this is probably the more courageous of the two.

The reaction of considering a man brave to become a stay at home Dad is particularly prevalent among women who have children. Do not allow this to worry you unduly, although obviously it should be a concern that those with experience of childcare should find an element of courage in your decision that you had possibly not previously considered.

However, of all the reactions you will get, this would seem to be one of the most intuitively accurate. Childcare is not an easy job for anybody (regardless of gender) and although being a stay at home Dad is different from being a stay at home mother it is continually surprising to me how many of the challenges are no different. They are just more noticeable because a stay at home Dad is not the norm. Issues that stay at home Dads will cite such as loneliness and isolation and the loss of a salary leading to financial constraints apply just as much to more traditional childcare arrangements.

ONGOING REACTION

Once the initial process of becoming a stay at home Dad is taken care of, you have to deal with the opinions of almost everybody you come into daily contact with. Once again, in most cases these tend to be positive, and include an element of envy regarding your fortunate position as a stay at home Dad.

Outside family and friends, the largest group you are likely to come into contact with is the community of stay at home mothers. Once again, opinions tend to be positive, but at times a man at home with the children will be treated with suspicion, as in some minds it is clear that something must be not quite right if Dad is looking after the children.

Occasionally you will come across what one stay at home father refers to as MWAs. Mothers With Attitude. These are the mothers who see you as an unwelcome element of diversity in the comfortable world of the mother and baby groups and the weekly clinic with the health visitor. In some ways it is possible to understand the reaction, as there are elements of the whole child rearing process that one can imagine a mother being uncomfortable discussing in the presence of a strange man, but it can cross the line and become active hostility to you personally.

MWAs need not necessarily be a problem, but one thing that

becomes clear very quickly is that almost all groups associated with children are somehow linked through the networks of mothers who attend them. A mother at one toddler group knows mothers at a Tiny Tumblers class, who in turn know mothers at another class, who know mothers at another toddler group. It is by linking into this network of mother and child activities that a lot of the fun and social interaction for both you and the children can be gained.

If you allow a mother with attitude to put you off and prevent you from joining this network then you and the kids will miss out on a lot. The vast majority of mothers are not like this and are often only too willing to go out of their way to involve the poor pathetic man with a child. (This may be condescending but take advantage of it, as it doesn't last long once they realise you're not as incapable as they expected you to be.)

In the end, whether you like it or not, there is a good chance that you will end up being treated as just another Mum. Having spent a very amusing few hours listening to a group of mothers go into some detail concerning their partners' failings, this is more fun than you can possibly imagine. There is also an immense feeling of relief at being a part of the discussion rather than the subject of it.

The majority of the opinions that people have of your decision to become a stay at home Dad will be modified by how they see you approach the task and deal with it on a daily basis. If you spend all your time telling people how you can't cope with the kids and how much you miss working for a living, they will quickly form the opinion that being a stay at home father was not a good decision for you or your family. Not too surprising really when you think about it.

If, however, you take a more positive and structured approach to the role, it is surprising how quickly the opinions of family and friends will become more positive. Close relatives especially need to be able to see that you are doing the right thing, in particular to ensure that your unusual home arrangements are meeting the needs of the children (despite the fact that you wouldn't even contemplate being a stay at home Dad if you thought this was a problem) and that what you are doing represents a positive vision of the future for you and your career.

In my experience, close relatives are happier with the idea that my situation is a temporary pragmatic solution, than with any thought that I may never return to work and normality again. It has been useful to be able to work on an occasional basis in order to be able to show that I am keeping my hand in for future job prospects, and many stay at home Dads find it useful to work part time for a variety of reasons.

The fact of the matter is that doing anything out of the ordinary generates a range of opinions and reactions. Being a stay at home Dad remains something out of the ordinary, and something that challenges many people's view of the world. It can make people concerned, uncomfortable, dismissive, and threatened. When it is people you can ignore, it is often useful to do so. But if it is close friends and family, then even though experience suggests they are normally supportive, it is up to you to show that this is the right thing, and that their concerns are unfounded. Eventually, even the most vocal opponents will grudgingly admit that your life isn't as bad as they thought it was when they see happy children and a stay at home Dad who is comfortable in his role.

Mental Stimulation

Despite the fact that, for the most part, being a stay at home Dad is an immensely satisfying and fulfilling experience, there are days when it can be very dull, and provide very little in the way of mental stimulation. In the early months, while they are undeniably cute and charming, kids don't actually do very much – at least not much that you can notice. Any expectation of playing football in the back garden in the first year just goes to show how little you knew about kids in the first place, and intelligent conversation seems to be out of the question for several years. (They also don't do much that doesn't require cleaning up after them, but that's another issue.)

As well as providing a salary, working for a living can be the source of most of our mental activity and stimulation. When you give this up, there are times when it feels as if the only difference between you and a house brick is that the house brick at least has other bricks to keep it company. Your level of mental activity may well be on a par.

UNREALISTIC PLANS

As I made plans to become a stay at home Dad I had no idea that this would be a problem. I had a list of all the things I was going to do with all the spare time I would have. After all, the small child I was looking after seemed to spend most of the day asleep, and when he wasn't asleep seemed to be happily entertained by the most basic of household objects. As long as I took a break from what I was doing every couple of hours to feed him then that would be fine, and we would all get along famously. These plans included:

1 Improving my rudimentary guitar playing beyond the point at which its development ceased some 20 years ago. I knew seven chords then and I know seven chords now. I can't be sure if they're the same seven chords, but seven seems to be about my limit.

2 Learning the piano beyond being able to play *Twinkle Twinkle Little Star*.

3 Catching up on all the great books I had never had time to read.

Unsurprisingly perhaps, none of these plans have come to fruition. There seem to be three main reasons for this (excluding my suspected genetic predisposition to idleness).

Firstly, you simply don't get the time you think you're going to. There is a whole lot of other stuff that needs to be done. Despite what you see on the television commercials, children will not happily entertain themselves all day with a £4.99 piece of plastic, however educational it is supposed to be. They won't feed or change themselves, however much you encourage them to, and they won't do all the housework. There are a lot of tasks that assume a priority above your own mental satisfaction and personal development.

Strangely, it wasn't long before I also realised that it was perhaps a little unreasonable for me to spend the day entertaining myself while my wife was out at work. It took even less time for my wife to point this fact out to me at some length. In fact, as she saw that I may have some time available, she helpfully left a list of home improvement tasks that she wanted doing on the front of the fridge. It was strange just how much of a full time occupation childcare became at that point.

Secondly, doing anything at all is difficult when children are involved. For a start, everything seems to take five times as long as it ought to. Actually it takes 25 times as long as it ought to. Just running the vacuum round the house (which at most should be a 20 minute task) there is a constant stream of interruptions as the toddler wants to use the vacuum cleaner, is frightened by the noise, wants to tell you something, stops you to point out that you missed a bit, needs to be taken to the toilet, or whatever else is essential to them just at that moment.

Any activity you do choose to undertake is immediately the most attractive thing in the house to a small child. If you read a book, they will want it, and if you play guitar, they will want to as well, and at an early age this isn't good for the guitar, or the child's fingers. Even when you get the chance to take advantage of a child's nap time, you can pretty well guarantee that they will wake up, cry, be disturbed, or for some reason or other find a way to prevent you ever completing a task.

The third main reason why these plans appear unlikely to come to fruition is that for long periods as a stay at home Dad, I have never been so tired in my life. All those times when I was going to do things while the baby took a nap I was on the bed next to the cot asleep as well.

Of course it is actually unreasonable to expect to be able to do all these things. The reason you are a stay at home Dad is to look after the children. You are not at home to do all the things you never got a chance to do because you were working all the time. Children need the stimulation, encouragement, support and guidance that a parent should be providing, and if you aren't doing this, then you're not doing the job properly. It is important to understand this before you start being a stay at home Dad and get rid of all those selfish plans for your own time as frankly you haven't got any of it anyway. You can't spend your time looking after the kids while wishing you were doing something else; that is a very effective recipe for frustration and eventual unhappiness.

MENTAL STAGNATION

Despite this, there is no getting away from the fact that looking after children full time does provide an ideal environment for mental stagnation. There are, of course, all those great moments with kids, but there are huge portions of time that are occupied by repetitive dull tasks that have to be done again and again. Washing, cleaning, feeding, changing, and all the other general care and maintenance activity.

Children's television provides little relief from this, and in the early years the toys hold little to interest the average adult either apart from wondering how on earth they justified that amount of money for three pieces of plastic. There is a temptation (that I succumbed to) to start to buy the toys you always wanted as a child. This is not normally a good idea. The toys that are of interest to you as a nostalgic visit to your younger years are almost invariably the toys that a small child can destroy in minutes. This is frustrating and expensive for all concerned.

AVOIDING MENTAL STAGNATION

There are some key things you need to avoid in order to prevent mental stagnation. These include:

- Staying in the house all day, as this provides too many opportunities to vegetate.

- Using television as a means to provide entertainment for the children. There are times when it is very tempting to sit them in front of the box and let them enjoy the pictures, but it is an illusion to think that this will give you the time to do other things. You are more likely to spend your time watching it with them. There is nothing more likely to induce the complete cessation of mental activity than kids' television. It can also be tempting to think that it will be all right to watch something you enjoy that will also entertain the child. Unfortunately television is reality, and when your two year old starts to behave like Tom and Jerry then you know this was a bad idea.

- Believing that you can maintain an intelligent conversation with a two year old. You can hold an enjoyable and fun conversation with a two year old, but trying to maintain your own mental faculties by using a small child as a sounding board will only confuse both of you.

KEEPING MENTALLY ACTIVE

As well as avoiding those things that induce mental stagnation, it is also important to find things that will keep your mind active. While many stay at home Dads will cite having more time to think as a benefit of being at home with the children, there is a limit to how much time anyone should spend effectively on their own thinking about things, especially if you have a tendency to watch television news or listen to life insurance commercials.

ACTIVITIES FOR MENTAL STIMULATION

- Your primary role is childcare, and although a large amount of this can at times seem to be intuitive, there is also an immense amount that can be learned regarding child development, physical health, and childcare techniques. There exists a vast library of material on childcare, ranging from the amusing to the downright dangerous. A desire to take the job of childcare seriously and professionally is a good enough enough reason to ensure you have a comprehensive knowledge of it. It is also very likely that at least some of the information will prove useful.

- Ensure that you have enough outside the house that can provide the mental stimulation you need. This can include childcare groups, local support groups, or any form or adult contact.

- If you have the opportunity to work part time this may ensure that you maintain an adequate level of mental activity.

- Plan trips and visits that will interest the children and you. One of the best (and free) days I ever spent with my son was at the Natural History Museum in London. He was happy to look at anything there, and it was also fascinating and educational for me.

I have found that it is important that *you* take on the task of providing mental stimulation for yourself, and don't rely on your partner to be able to provide a full day's worth of mental sparring in the evening. You may well have spent all day thinking about things that you now need to get off your chest and involve her in intense intellectual discussion, but she has been at work all day and, frankly, probably isn't in the mood for anything other than a quick rundown on what the kids did, a long bath, and a quiet dinner.

It is worth emphasising however that every day is (normally) full of delightful moments. A first word, a first sentence, a first joke (invariably not very funny to anyone other than you and your child), the first time they do a puzzle, or they learn to count, are great moments. The greatest mental stimulation you can hope for can be obtained from developing the skills that will enable you to help your children to learn and develop as happy children. This requires real dedication, skill, and thought on your part, as well as the patience of a saint and the awareness to recognise when they have had enough, and when you are in danger of turning your child into a performing monkey just to keep you amused during the day.

As an aside, one additional area where some mental activity has provided a nice joint project for both my wife and me, has been to try and improve our fluency in a foreign language. This has not only been an enjoyable activity, but it also has the immediate benefit of providing a way to communicate sensitive information to one another (e.g. that it's bathtime) in the presence of a toddler who seems to hear everything we say.

Although there are days when being a stay at home Dad can seem to be just a long round of boring repetitive tasks, it doesn't have to be like this. The tasks will not go away, but they can all be made fun (even nappy changing) and by establishing a regular routine and getting organised there is no reason why these essential tasks should ever make you feel that is all there is to being a stay at home Dad. Once again, it is up to you to enter into the role with the enthusiasm and commitment that you gave to your career. (OK, maybe a bit more enthusiasm and commitment than you gave to your career.)

Avoiding mental stagnation is important for a stay at home Dad, and maintaining a range of outside interests within the constraints of the childcare role is important, but the primary focus has to be on obtaining mental stimulation from the day to day activity of looking after children. You can do this by getting involved in the childcare community that exists, and by approaching your role as a stay at home Dad in a professional and organised way.

Friends

Children should carry a health warning. Actually they should carry several health warnings, but one of them would be that children could seriously damage your social life. If you become a stay at home Dad they can damage your social life more than you can possibly imagine, from the very moment you start to be a stay at home Dad.

The day that you become a stay at home Dad means you have probably just left your place of work for the last time. Leaving work quite probably means leaving behind a significant portion of your social life. Many of us first meet our friends through our work, and a lot of people meet their partner through work as well.

WORK COLLEAGUES

When you give up work you are leaving all this behind. There are no more drinks after work, no more corporate golf days, no more colleagues to get to know on business trips and no more daily contact of office life. Not only can it feel as if you are you losing your old friends at work; it may also seem that you are also losing the potential to make new friends.

When you first leave work you may well have a mental list of colleagues who have become friends whom you would expect to keep in touch with and maintain some kind of social interaction with. It is a sad fact of life but once you are no longer at work every day, the majority of these people will move on without you. They will have new people to impress, new groups to work with and new things to do. Things will change at the office, and soon the only contribution you will ever be able to make to a conversation will be that "we didn't do things that way when I was there." This means that you become very boring very quickly.

For some ex-colleagues your leaving results in a situation even worse than this. They can see your departure from work as a form of betrayal, and ironically it can be those whom you were closest to at work who feel this the most. You had been a part of their personal support network, and part of the group of people whom they felt comfortable with, and by leaving you are somehow letting them down and denying the values and commitments that you shared with them. Some may feel that you no longer value their friendship.

The truth is that however much you try and continue with work relationships they are just not the same once you have left. The shared experience soon fades into memory, and while nostalgic reminiscences around the log fire can be fun once in a while they do not represent the same basis for a supportive and active friendship as being involved in the daily thrills and spills of office life. Experience would suggest that it is the exception rather than the rule for even relatively close work relationships to be sustained once the basis of that relationship has been removed.

MAINTAINING A SOCIAL LIFE

Becoming a stay at home Dad can also seriously damage your social life in other ways. It is not a nine to five job, so it is always difficult to commit to regular social events or participation in clubs and societies that may be where you count your friends. It is not always possible to be able to hand over the children to your partner the moment she walks into the house after a long day at work.

For a start, even if she does get home at a reasonable hour, it is quite possible that she is exhausted and stressed and perhaps a two year old climbing up her green silk suit isn't the best thing in the world. It is also possible that your partner may be away on business, working late at the office, or have enough work in the briefcase she brought home with her to keep her busy until tomorrow morning. You don't necessarily get evenings off as a stay at home Dad.

Even having a social life with your partner can be more difficult than you might imagine. Finding a reliable babysitter whom you're prepared to trust with your children is not easy. Of course part of the reason for this is that we seem to be developing an increasingly paranoid style of parenting, but hey, just because you're a paranoid parent doesn't mean your babysitter isn't out to get you.

When you do have a babysitter there remain constraints on an evening out. Gone are the two bottles of wine and a taxi home. As soon as you get home after an evening out, one of you may well have to drive the babysitter home and, what's more, just because it's midnight doesn't mean you're off duty. Since becoming a stay at home Dad I have reduced my alcohol intake to a fraction of what it was. (Quite a small fraction in fact.) It just wasn't worth the feeling of hell as you try to deal with a screaming child while suffering the after effects of the night before.

OLD FRIENDS

As well as your work friends and your partner, there are of course all those old friends whom you keep in touch with and go to stay with every once in a while. Surely having children won't have an adverse impact on those relationships? However, getting away to stay with these lifelong friends becomes more complicated when you have children, especially if your friends don't have children of their own. It's a major effort to get away in the first place, involving taking more equipment and supplies than most polar expeditions, all loaded into the boot of the car, in the space beneath the seats, and on the roof. As soon as you get there you discover that this apparently wasn't enough and the kids are bored and fractious because they haven't got all their toys or they wanted to bring their friends with them. At bedtime, just as you're looking forward to a bottle of red wine and a chat about old times, they become increasingly disturbed as they realise they're not going home and they are going to have to sleep in a strange bed.

At this point you realise that you're also on edge because the kids don't know this house, and the eldest might be sleepwalking and there are no stairgates and the whole house is actually a death trap for anyone under the age of 18. Every room is full of danger, and not just the monsters hiding in the wardrobe. Power points, glass ornaments, electric heaters, the toilet, and the toilet seat; they all carry the potential for disaster. You know that the kids will be up all night, so you don't have a drink; you and your partner become very boring company, as your hosts get increasingly drunk in order to deal with the stress of your happily anticipated visit. The only good news is that you won't be invited again.

Friends with children may seem a much better option, except that few people have houses that can accommodate two full families, and at the point when all the kids are fighting over the same toy and asking when they're leaving, you realise that perhaps you did in fact enjoy the weekend you spent with your childless friends, because it was so much better than this.

Despite all this, for the stay at home Dad, being able to maintain some existing friendships and making new friends is essential to be able to thrive and survive in the role. These friends tend to fall into two distinct categories. Firstly there are the 'man friends' and then there are the 'baby related' friends.

SOMETHING MANLY

Most stay at home Dads will tell you that, without the usual outlet provided by work, and having spent most of the day being fully domesticated and house trained, it does inspire the need to go and do something manly on a regular basis. This could be just meeting mates down the pub, playing sport, or some other suitably masculine hobby or pastime. Whatever it is, it is an essential antidote to a day of nappy sacks and washing machines.

Being a stay at home Dad is not necessarily an indication that you are in desperate need of getting in touch with your feminine side. In my particular case, this need for some kind of manly activity and male company was met by playing soccer and golf, and indulging in outrageously ambitious DIY projects that involved much grunting and knocking things down, but I suspect that taking the car apart would have done just as well. Anything that creates a lot of mess and involves the use of power tools would seem to suffice.

BABY RELATED FRIENDS

For baby related friends the really good news is that if someone wanted to invent a way to meet other people they would invent children. They are the ideal subject of first time conversation and a great icebreaker in any social gathering. Everyone seems to want to make a comment about a child; any parent is only too willing to bore the pants off anyone they meet on the subject of their own children, and two toddlers in a room tend not to need a formal introduction.

The easiest and most obvious way to get to meet people and make friends with others who have children is through the plethora of toddler groups and parenting groups that exist in almost any area. You can make some preparation for becoming a stay at home Dad by attending antenatal classes or any other organised events for new parents with your partner. This is particularly beneficial as you meet people who may be going through exactly the same emotions as you are, having recently given up work and acquired a small child at the same time. This is useful because you are dealing with the same child related issues at the same time, providing a source of interesting and useful conversation as you compare developmental progress, think about play groups, schools, or the general illnesses that seem to strike all children at similar stages in their life. (Note however that when comparing developmental progress, raising a child is not a competition, and everybody's child is particularly advanced for their age as far as they are concerned.)

My personal experience has been that attending groups with your partner while she is on maternity leave is particularly beneficial. Most of the people you will meet at toddler groups and in any daytime event involving children are likely to be women. I don't perceive myself as a particularly frightening individual, but there is, sadly, an inevitable level of suspicion that any man in this environment seems to attract. The mothers with whom I was initially able to communicate without this suspicion were those who had also met my wife. Somehow I was a safer individual because of it, perhaps because they knew I hadn't borrowed a child just to be able to get into the toddler group.

Friends tend to create friends, and if you can make the initial break-through and make a few friends from antenatal classes or toddler groups, then this will naturally create a wider circle of acquaintances as you get to meet their friends and acquaintances. The main way to achieve this is to make sure you get out and about in the places where you are likely to meet people on an ad hoc basis, along with one of your existing friends. Just by being there and being with a child, once the initial suspicion passes you almost invariably acquire the fascina-tion for them that comes with your novelty value as a stay at home Dad. By being in the same places at the same time it is surprising how soon you start to see the same people, and soon conversation becomes inevitable. Also, you should always accept an invitation to any child's birthday party, as once again this is a great way to get to meet more parents and spend more time with them.

The friends you make through your child are important as they pro-vide willing sources of advice, potential babysitting arrangements, and just someone to whinge to when that is the only thing that seems to help. Nobody knows everything there is to know about bringing up children, and it is a comfort to see mothers in the same situation as you with the same questions and the same challenges. They may sometimes seem to have all the answers, as they serenely go about their day, but just like ducks and just like you, underneath the surface they are paddling furiously too. It's nice to see that as a stay at home Dad you're probably not doing as bad a job as you might have thought.

There are some dangers that you need to be aware of. Firstly, as you become friendly with the mothers you meet during your daily exis-tence there is nothing to say that you are also going to get on with their partners. This could be a potential source of conflict in the future if you do not hit it off with them. Secondly, I have found it important to involve your own partner as much as possible in these relationships. This is not because there is any danger of illicit relationships, or even the suspicion of any illicit relationships, but it is essential that you don't exclude her. This is especially so, as these friendships are likely to be accompanied by friendships between your children and those of your new friends. If your partner is excluded from these relationships, she is also excluded from your children's friendships.

By building new friendships you are not only extending your own circle of friends; you are extending your children's circle of friends as well. Cultivating a wide circle of child related friends is important for the stay at home Dad and important for the kids and your partner as well.

As you settle into a role as a primary carer, you will discover a whole new range of friends and acquaintances through the children. This will include the prospective parents you meet through whatever antenatal classes you attend, and then the parents of your children's friends. Maintaining existing friendships can become more difficult, particularly if they involve long distance travelling or they were based on a work relationship that you are no longer a part of, but it is surprising how quickly some of these become just a distant memory.

Status and Perks

There are lots of people for whom status is important. It is a reflection of how successful they are and how much respect is accorded to them. Status is about what people think of them. The status of the people they meet reflects on them.

THE STATUS OF WORK

A lot of status can come from your job. There is the financial status of a good salary, the status of the new company car, the status of working for a living, and the status of wearing a suit and tie. While you could potentially continue to wear a suit and tie as a stay at home Dad it would be an exceptionally stupid thing to do, and there's no denying that when you become a stay at home Dad the normal status symbols and the ancillary perks of the job are taken away from you one by one. The good news is that they are replaced by something much more rewarding.

When you first give up work it can be something of a shock to realise just how much of your life was tied to your employer. It is also something of a surprise how easy it is to live without most of it as well.

Giving up a salary is an issue for every family that goes from two incomes to one, regardless of who stays at home to look after the kids. For Dad however, giving up things such as the company car may be more difficult. However, it is clear that the car you needed for work (or indeed the car you needed before you had children) is not the one you need now. What you need now is five doors, a lot of boot space, and upholstery that won't mind chocolate, sick, apple juice, more sick, mud and, finally, more sick being spread all over it in copious amounts. Metallic paint just isn't that important any more, and you don't need to be spending many thousands of pounds on a new car when the furthest you're going to travel in it is the supermarket. You can be fairly sure however that your new car will accurately reflect the status you now have in society.

THE STATUS OF A STAY AT HOME DAD

As a stay at home Dad you have little or no status at all. To some extent you are a complete non-person, in that nobody really knows how to react to you. (As an aside you also no longer appear in official statistics, except under the offensively dismissive category of 'economically inactive'. Actually we're just a sub-group of economically inactive. We don't even rate our own category.)

Quite often you will find you need to introduce yourself as "I'm a stay at home father, but I used to be x" where x will give the people you meet some idea as to who you are and how they feel they should respond to you. Most people have not come across many stay at home fathers and have little idea about how to react, and certainly no idea whether you deserve the status reserved for gentry or whether you are in fact a complete deadbeat who was just lucky enough to have a partner with a career.

It can be quite liberating for all the trappings of a career to be removed and to reinvent yourself as a stay at home father, even though in this role you are not perceived as an important person by anyone outside your family. To the majority of people you will meet you are just another parent, and it doesn't matter whether you are the father or the mother. You certainly no longer influence people's careers, you don't get to write their appraisals, or determine their annual bonus payment. For some reason the invitations to corporate entertainment events seem to dry up as well.

At the same time, it can also be upsetting when you get the sensation of everyone around you progressing in their career, acquiring the latest gadgets, flying to exotic locations, and being promoted into the job that should have been yours.

One of the most interesting experiences I have had as a stay at home Dad has been to accompany my partner to a social event held for senior staff in her organisation. This was fascinating at several levels in that the majority of the people who worked there were male, so the majority of the partners were female. While they didn't go as far as presenting me with flowers, it was clear from some of the arrangements that they were unsure what to do with me. There seemed to be an initial assumption that I was a staff member they hadn't met before, but as it became known around the party that I had given up work to become a stay at home Dad I think the esteem in which my wife was held went up measurably. Here was a woman so dedicated to her career that she had managed to persuade her husband to give up his job to stay at home. Being a stay at home Dad may not immediately enhance your status but it may do wonders for the status of your partner. Being the supportive one in the background doesn't carry a lot of kudos in most circumstances but it is something you have to get used to as a stay at home Dad.

Even when you are working part time you have to to accept that as the primary carer your career is secondary to your partner's and to the needs of the children. At this particular event it was soon impossible for me to have a conversation that did not involve the complexities of childcare and the intricacies of household appliances. I felt I had a wider contribution to make to many of the conversations, but once you are pigeonholed as a stay at home Dad that's what you seem to be allowed to talk about.

How people react to you, and the importance they associate with you in your role are perhaps two of the elements of working for a living that I do miss. Some stay at home Dads get the impression that what they are doing is viewed as nothing more than a hobby or a temporary aberration that they will get over soon enough. The basically patronising reactions that you often get to the news of what you do with your days are a reflection of the lack of importance that people associate with the role of a primary carer. I am sure this must get to women who have given up work to look after the kids as well.

THE PERKS OF BEING A STAY AT HOME DAD

However, it has to be said that in many areas the status and perks of being a stay at home Dad greatly outweigh anything that you have to leave behind when you stop going to the office. For many men you acquire the status of being a very lucky man. Whether you choose to believe this or not doesn't really matter, and it can be tempting to start reading articles about 'superdads' and believing it all applies to you, and that yes, you can have it all. Most stay at home Dads will tell you that they feel very fortunate to be able to spend the time they can with the children, but it is not for everyone, and the status of lucky man can be just a result of an unrealistic perception of what being a stay at home Dad involves.

As a stay at home Dad you also acquire the status accorded to your novelty value, particularly with some of the mothers you meet as a result of your childcare activities. While this novelty value is possibly the equivalent of being a vaudeville act involving singing chickens, it is normally a real compliment to be involved in activities in which the usual participants are just the mums, and there is great pleasure to be gained from being accepted as part of a circle of friends. Most stay at home Dads find toddler groups initially daunting, but perseverance proves worthwhile for most of them, and they have provided friendship, support, and a social life for Dad and the children.

However, regardless of the status that you achieve as a stay at home Dad, it still doesn't come with a company car, gym membership or an expense account. Some of the perks it does deliver however include:

- The opportunity to see your children develop, and to play the most active part imaginable in their development.
- The opportunity to be more involved in local organisations, events and activities.
- The opportunity to become involved in voluntary work, support groups and the like.
- The opportunity to have more time to spend with other family members such as your parents.
- The chance not to shave, dress in a suit and tie, commute to work, or sit in a cubicle like a battery hen all day.
- More time to think.

Most stay at home Dads don't particularly miss the work environment; the aspects of work they miss tend to be the social and psychological benefits of working for living rather than the perks that are associated with a job. The perks that are associated with being a stay at home Dad have the additional advantage of changing over time. The fun things of looking after a baby change into the fun things of looking after a toddler. The fun of looking after just one child becomes a different kind of fun when you have more than one. When you are in the garden playing football at 7.30 on a summer's morning rather than sitting on a train or crawling on the motorway, you know that the perks of being a stay at home Dad make any of the perks you had as part of your job pale into insignificance.

If you are missing your company perks you can comfort yourself with the knowledge that even if you still had access to the perks of working for a living they wouldn't help anyway. You would still have to have the family option for the company car, you would never get time to go to the gym, and the idea of a long lunch in a restaurant is soon just a memory, and not nearly as much fun as a picnic with the kids in tow.

When you're out in the countryside on a sunny day with a bag full of sandwiches, 'economically inactive' doesn't sound like the worst thing you can be.

Acting the Professional

When you first stop working to become a stay at home Dad it may seem as if you have given up the mantle of professional life and you can happily abandon everything that went with it. Out goes the suit, the tie, shaving every morning, reading the appalling trade press, worrying about impressing the boss, and all those other things that were so annoying. However, when this happy thought occurs, there are two things you should remember.

1 You may well need to return to your professional life at some point.
2 You will continue to experience everything associated with the world of work through your partner and, surprisingly, in some ways living it vicariously can be worse than doing it yourself.

Being a stay at home Dad may be the most important thing you've ever done, and it may be the most lasting contribution you ever make to society. (After 20 years working in the telecommunications industry I recently had the unfortunate realisation that every product I had ever worked on had now been discontinued or made obsolete.) As this is the most important thing you have ever done, it should be obvious that this task needs to be approached with as much professionalism and enthusiasm as anything you ever did in the office – preferably more.

If you can put your heart and soul into the meaningless tasks that your intellectually challenged boss asked you to perform, then the least you can do is satisfy every whim of an irate toddler.

Taking care of kids is a major task. I know lots of people do it, and they all seem to get on with it without too much trouble, but it is still an activity that is fraught with pitfalls and unique challenges. It is important to treat the job in a professional way. This is what you do now. You are a stay at home Dad. If you are spending your time thinking about other things or wishing you were doing something else then you need to make a serious readjustment. Surprisingly, working for a living and acquiring a professional skill has given you some capability that can be reused in childcare.

APPLYING PROFESSIONAL SKILLS

Meeting management is an essential childcare skill. A huge amount of time is spent in some kind of meeting or other, from Mother and Baby clubs, through to weekly clinic visits, doctor's appointments, school visits, and a host of other things. They can all be improved by being given the same professional treatment that any meeting in the office should. Knowing what you want from a meeting with the health visitor, and having a written agenda, ensures that everything you want to discuss actually gets discussed.

Researching the subject and completing staff work can be applied to the role of a stay at home Dad. With a first child everyone, regardless of gender, feels somewhat lost. Researching the subject fully and reading everything you can on the subject will help to increase the knowledge that provides confidence and competence when dealing with the mechanics of childcare. Of course the majority of these books are in the most part written by women for stay at home mothers, and assume that Dad is at best only marginally involved in the childcare process. Life is too short to be irritated by this. Babies appear to be fairly similar regardless of whether it is Mum or Dad who is looking after them.

It is also worth using your professional approach to work in setting objectives and measuring your own achievement. It is easy to drift from day to day when the majority of the day is occupied by the practicalities of looking after children. By planning the week ahead, and planning the day's activities with some kind of objective, you can guard against drifting aimlessly or failing to do what is needed for both you and the children. These objectives do not need to be particularly complicated or require sophisticated measurement systems.

In my case I had very simple objectives that included:

• Visit at least one local friend for coffee every week.
• Visit the local library once a week.
• Get out of the house every day.
• Do some exercise every day.
• Do at least one class every week.
• Cook proper healthy meals.

If you want to take measurement very seriously it is possible to compare yourself against the professional childcare community by using the same government criteria to analyse what you are doing, but this may be taking it to an extreme.

Budget management is another key professional skill to bring to the home, especially as it is bizarre how much money we all waste as a result of being at work and not having the time or the inclination to sort out the best deal. Telephone, electricity, gas and many other services all seem to be priced on the basis that there is a huge inertia that stops anyone from ever changing supplier. It is almost certainly possible that by taking a professional approach to the household financial outgoings, you can save money.

Perhaps the most important skill, particularly when multiple children are involved, is that of project management. Almost every task becomes a major project in some way when children are involved. By managing tasks in a professional way, the irritation and annoyance of everything taking five times longer than it used to can be reduced. With children small problems quickly become major issues. Something seemingly as trivial as forgetting to take a favourite toy on holiday can be the end of a happy family vacation. Anything that might help to avoid this has got to be worth a try.

Other skills that can be useful include:

• Presentation skills; "That's not broccoli, it's a new food you'll really like."
• Assertiveness: "You will eat that broccoli."
• Conflict resolution: "Let's understand your issue with broccoli."
• Crisis management: "There's no need to choke on the broccoli."

Becoming a stay at home Dad is not the beginning of life as one long lazy Sunday morning. Even though you are leaving the professional work environment behind, it is the way in which you approach the role of a stay at home Dad that will be the major contributing factor to the quality of the home you establish for your children. As a job it exceeds the responsibility and difficulty of most other jobs, and needs to be approached with the level of professionalism that it deserves. It is not without its challenges.

NEW SKILLS REQUIRED

Although there are some aspects of the stay at home Dad role that seem to come naturally to most fathers, and there are parts of the role for which you are somewhat equipped as a result of your experience gained while working, there are also significant portions of the role that will require you to gain some new skills fairly quickly. In particular this will include medical diagnosis of common childhood complaints, behavioural analysis, developmental milestone analysis, entertainment, teaching, cooking, becoming a soccer coach, dance instructor, musician, singer, life coach, personal trainer, and a range of other things. These are all in addition to the basic physical tasks of fetching, carrying, driving, picking up, cleaning, washing, dressing, and responding to any particular whim of the moment.

Anyone who tells you that looking after children isn't a full time occupation that needs to be approached professionally clearly isn't doing the job properly.

THE IMPORTANCE OF A PROFESSIONAL APPROACH

Taking the professionalism that is normally reserved for the workplace and applying it to the role of a stay at home Dad can be important to you in several ways.

1 It helps to maintain a sense of the importance and the complexity of the role.
2 It can help to define the role in a way that provides structure to your daily life.
3 It provides a way of dealing with an unfamiliar role by using familiar techniques.

As a stay at home Dad you will be subject to more scrutiny than is normal in terms of how you are approaching your childcare role and how it is affecting the children. This scrutiny may come from family and friends, healthcare professionals, or just the people you meet in the street. If you can show that you are taking a professional approach to your role, and that giving up work has not immediately caused you to become a disorganised slob in jogging pants, this will go some way to satisfying the self-appointed scrutinisers of your performance.

MAINTAINING PROFESSIONALISM AS A STAY AT HOME DAD

Maintaining a level of professionalism to satisfy everyone who thinks that being a stay at home Dad is a strange thing to do means that you have to work hard at it. To maximise the impression of professionalism you should:

1 Define a long term plan for your role as a stay at home Dad.
2 Establish a routine that includes preparing for the day in the same way as if you were going out to work.
3 Show a professional approach to all aspects of the role, including running the house, managing finances, and managing time.
4 Set objectives for yourself and ensure there are defined activities for the kids.
5 Show that you understand key developmental milestones for the children.
6 Understand how external organisations measure their performance with children, for example, standards for childminders or day nurseries.
7 Be aware of when you start to take short cuts or act with a lower level of professionalism. Keeping a diary can help to show trends in behaviour.
8 Become proficient in the new skills required for your role as a stay at home Dad.

By taking a professional approach to the role of a stay at home Dad you will:

- Feel more comfortable with what you are doing and more confident in your ability to do it.

- Look more professional and capable to those who are judging your performance as a stay at home Dad.

- Be more switched on to the attitudes and capabilities that will be required should you choose to return to work.

- Provide a better experience for your children.

PROFESSIONALISM AND YOUR PARTNER

Maintaining a sense of professionalism is also important in maintaining your relationship with your partner. While you are busy being a stay at home Dad your partner is still going out to work every day, being a professional person in the adult world. Every day she is exposed to the real world, and the attributes that are required to be successful in that world. Being able to burp the alphabet isn't one of them.

The level of professionalism you show in your role as a stay at home Dad will inevitably affect her view of you as a person, your suitability for providing childcare for her children, and how your role is impacting on you. She is likely to be more worried than most that you are going to find it difficult to adjust to your role and that you will be unhappy with a life of nappies and formula milk. By being professional about the role you can help to reduce these worries.

It is also worth bearing in mind that she will be spending the day in the company of smartly dressed, highly motivated, exciting and ambitious young men who don't smell of baby vomit. She will not necessarily want to return home each evening to someone who appears to have completely lost not only the plot, but also any self-respect they once had. While I'm not sure you need to be greeting her at the door in a tuxedo while proffering a dry martini I think some effort is required.

By acting the professional you can help her to see that you are doing the job properly, taking a serious approach to it, and that the job of being a stay at home Dad is providing an arena where you can use your skills to the full.

By keeping your daily activities on the same intellectual level as your partner's working life, rather than allowing your day to become a soul sapping series of tedious domestic chores, you can stay on the same wavelength as your partner in conversation. This is important, as an integral part of the role of a stay at home Dad is to provide a supportive and listening ear as your partner tells you all about her day at the office in excruciating, gut wrenching, irrelevant detail. Despite the fact that you no longer go to work every day, you are fortunate enough to now have the inestimable pleasure of experiencing it vicariously as you hear about your partner's day.

Any desire to interrupt her and tell her about how you finally figured out the washing machine, and how many nappies you changed today, should be resisted at all costs. It's not about you any more. An integral part of the role of the stay at home Dad is to listen attentively while your partner provides a full review of her day. This is, perhaps, one of the most frustrating experiences known to man. Listening to the intricacies of her project schedules and staffing levels, a part of me can feel a wistful longing for the days when I dealt with grown-up problems and had grown-up arguments with grown-up people. I suspect my wife can detect some of this frustration, and she tries to involve me by asking my advice on particular problems she may be experiencing at work. Unfortunately, three years of separation from the work environment has caused my opinions to become more extreme, and my advice less useful.

Away from the practicalities of day to day office life, my answer to every staffing problem is to sack them, and any customer issue can be resolved by telling the customer to either stop being such a pain or to find another supplier. It is fortunate for her employers that my wife has ceased to take seriously anything I say.

This is one of many changes that have made me realise that three years as a stay at home Dad has quite probably now left me completely unemployable. Dealing with a toddler seems to require a simplistic black and white approach to life. Things are right or wrong; good or bad; nice or nasty. There are no shades of grey. I suppose I could take this attitude back into the workplace one day, but I can't imagine it being the foundation for rapid career progression or harmonious relationships with colleagues.

So, while there are some things I miss about being in a professional working environment, it is probably the case that I couldn't do it again right now. Even if I could, I wouldn't want to. The days of a stay at home Dad can be long and they can be filled with unexciting and repetitive tasks. The shopping has to be done, the clothes have to be washed, and the dust in our house appears to have evolved to become a self-reproducing organism. It is some comfort to remember that life in the office is also full of dull and repetitive tasks, and while a professional approach can help as a stay at home Dad, going back to work would also require missing out on so much at home.

Taking a professional approach to the role and using techniques with which you are familiar can help you to deal with some of the daily issues you face by placing them in a context you are comfortable with. Looking and feeling professional can also help the way you feel about yourself and your role, and show those around you that you aren't just on an extended vacation, but that you're taking a serious approach to a serious responsibility.

Being Part of a Tribe

For many people their job or their vocation is a big part of their sense of personal identity, and provides a sense of belonging to a specific group. This may be their professional group, and also their company, and many companies spend a lot of time and money trying to ensure their staff feel a sense of belonging to the organisation, at least until they make them redundant.

The process of working can provide an important structure to our lives. It can provide a set of shared values, in many careers a specific language of its own, common objectives to be achieved, rewards and compensation, public accolades, and all the benefits of being a part of a community.

There is a huge amount of comfort and security to be obtained from being part of a structured group when you are working for a living. When you become a stay at home Dad, this doesn't exist in such an obvious form.

In some ways this particular challenge is not dissimilar to that faced by those who retire from a long career with a company, those who are unlucky enough to be made redundant, or those who choose to leave the cocoon of corporate life in order to strike out on their own in a flash of entrepreneurial enthusiasm. However, as a stay at home Dad you may not have any involvement in the world of work which you would as an entrepreneur, and you can't spend all day on the golf course like many a retired person.

BEING ON YOUR OWN

There is a real danger that as a stay at home Dad you will suddenly find yourself out on your own for the first time in your life. You're not a part of a school, university or a corporate entity. The chances are that you have belonged to some sort of grouping like that since you were four or five years old. For some this may be a completely liberating experience, but for others it can take away a lot of the structure and organisation that they have come to depend on. (Ah, so that's why I was going to work all those years, even when I hated it!)

There is at least one incidence I know of a stay at home Dad who, having left work to look after the children, spent early morning and early evening hanging around the entrance to the office so he could still feel a part of what was going on and keep up with the office gossip, and there are more frequent examples of stay at home Dads continuing to use email and the world wide web to maintain contact with the organisations they have recently left.

WAS IT DIFFICULT TO GIVE UP WORK?

Some stay at home Dads have found it very easy to give up work, but for others it has represented a significant and difficult change for a number of reasons:

1 Their career had just become established and they could see their future career path that was now no longer available to them.

2 They had invested a lot of time in building a good reputation in their organisation that would now be lost.

3 There were concerns that the skills acquired in their career would now be wasted and be outdated by the time they returned to work.

4 There were concerns that they would find it difficult to re-enter the workplace.

5   They enjoyed working and were definitely taking on their role as a stay at home Dad on a temporary basis and would be returning to work as soon as possible.

MISSING THE OFFICE

As part of the preparation for leaving work it is important to create a substitute for some of the non-financial benefits of going to work, that can provide you with the same support and feelings of belonging that you had when you were a valuable contributing member of society. Working as a full time childcare provider is very different from being in the office, and although on the whole there is no way I would go back (unless I am dragged kicking and screaming, or told to by my wife) there are things that the office provides that you may find you will start to miss.

WHAT STAY AT HOME DADS MISS ABOUT WORK

1   The thrill of delivering something for a customer.
2   The excitement of making money or doing a deal.
3   The social interaction.
4   Financial security.
5   Job responsibility.
6   Recognition of contributions by colleagues.
7   A pat on the back for a job well done.

I didn't think it would happen to me, and it's a difficult thing to admit, but there are days when I do actually miss the office. I can't claim that I miss the work, but it is the aspects of the office environment that gave a sense of belonging and contributed to the working experience, that seem a lot more attractive in retrospect. Particularly when I don't have to go there any more.

Firstly, there is the time spent with other adults. It is nice to be able to have a conversation without being on your hands and knees. It's even nicer to be able to have a conversation that doesn't include only the word "Why?" as the sole response to everything you say. This can easily turn into an unhealthy craving for adult company. Any adult company will do. The postman doesn't like coming to our house any more.

Secondly, there is the time spent without children being around. This is different from being with adults. Just the absence of children can be a refreshing experience. However wonderful your child, living with them 24 hours a day is in some ways proof that it is possible to have too much of a good thing.

Thirdly, there is the fact that working for a living at least gives you something in common with most other people. One of the biggest problems with being the primary carer is that you soon discover that you only have one subject of conversation. While the state of my child's nappies may be a subject of fundamental importance to my life, no other member of the male sex really wants to hear about it. Some of my male friends seem to think I'm some kind of lazy dead-beat who watches TV all day and really needs to get off my backside, get a job, and stop sponging off my poor wife.

The work environment provides a set of common experiences that are the basis for a lot of conversation. Childcare provides a set of experiences that don't represent acceptable subjects for the dinner table. While those around me are discussing the latest moves in the office, the business trip to Vienna, and what colour BMW they think they'll get, all I can contribute is something about the cost of children's shoes. Once you're a stay at home Dad you don't get invited to many dinner parties any more, which is just as well because you can never find a babysitter anyway.

The final, and in some ways the most difficult part of the change to deal with, is that there are no day to day congratulations for a job well done. While a successful trip to the potty does have its own particular kind of job satisfaction, expecting a small child to give you the occasional pat on the back and tell you what a good job you're doing is probably unreasonable. They're more likely to throw a tantrum and tell you how much they hate you, and want their mother. The motivational skills of a two year old are not particularly well developed, but can be effective in their own way.

The chances are that there isn't a lot of praise and congratulations forthcoming from your partner either. For some unfathomable reason my wife even gets slightly annoyed when I start fishing for praise just because I ran the dishwasher and managed to get the vacuum cleaner out of the cupboard. It's possible I should have waited until she had taken her coat off after a 10 hour day at work and an hour's journey home, but I was so proud of myself it simply couldn't wait.

To add to this lack of recognition of a job well done, it also seems that nobody puts any real value on the role of the full time childcarer any more. The government seems obsessed with trying to make everyone spend all their time in the office rather than raising their children, and even the mothers I know who have taken time off from work to bring up their children feel they should be back at work, and many of them are counting the days until they can start making a contribution again.

When those doing the childcaring seem to be convinced that a more valuable activity would be to become an admin assistant somewhere, then there is something seriously wrong.

HOW CAN YOU REPLACE THE FEELING OF BELONGING THAT WORK CAN PROVIDE?

Finding something to replace the peripheral benefits of working for a living, and the feeling of belonging to a group, can be important and there are several ways stay at home Dads have approached this.

- Becoming active in the voluntary childcare support groups that exist around the country.
- Becoming involved in some of the internet based virtual communities that exist, for example, homedad.org (www.homedad.org.uk) that is specifically targeted at stay at home fathers. Some are also regularly involved in the internet communities targeted at stay at home mothers. Nobody knows you're a stay at home Dad on the internet.
- Developing local groups and contacts with other stay at home fathers to arrange days out or just informal gatherings.
- Joining clubs and societies not associated with childcare to develop a hobby or pastime.

Although the majority of stay at home fathers claim not to miss working for a living, there is a significant minority who feel a large part of their life is missing, and however many clubs and societies you join or however involved you become in local and national organisations, there are aspects of working for a living for which it is difficult to find a direct substitute.

In my own case it has particularly been the sense of progression, and a feeling of growth and development that has been missing. While the days are busy, the pace of life feels slower, and it can feel as if the rest of the world went past while you were changing the baby, and in reality your role represents just a break from the normal life that you will resume when the kids finally get off to school.

However, as a stay at home Dad you need to remember that you belong to a very elite group, doing a job that is probably the most satisfying thing you will ever do, as well as quite possibly the most challenging. You are part of a growing group of stay at home Dads and part of a huge group of stay at home parents who have made the choice to provide parental care for their children. You may have lost some of the sense of belonging that working for a living provided, but there is a whole new world that you are now a part of, and a whole new dress code that you will have to learn.

Looking the Part

The uniform and clothes that provide the outward signs of the working tribe to which you belong are another aspect of the office life that (unbelievable as it may sound) you can miss. After 20 years of wearing a suit and tie to the office every day I was genuinely enthused by the prospect of wearing casual clothes instead. It was unfortunate that I didn't own any. At least not any that were suitable for dealing with a small child.

THE IMPORTANT THINGS ABOUT CLOTHES

After three years I have come to the conclusion that there are six important factors to consider with clothes:

1 They must be comfortable and loose. There is enough that is annoying throughout the day, without adding uncomfortable clothes to the list.

2 They must fit in a way that is decent in any number of the strange positions required for lifting, carrying, or otherwise dealing with a small person. This is particularly important for a stay at home Dad as I spend most of my time as the only male in a female dominated world. I am not suggesting that a glimpse of my underwear is likely to affect young mothers everywhere by releasing a fury of repressed passion, but it is likely to cause some concern in a public environment, when the man is flashing his underwear at every opportunity.

3 They must not contain zips, buttons, or anything else likely to be of interest to, or inflict scratches on, a small child. The second worst injury my son has had in two years was caused by carrying him on my hip while wearing a pair of trousers with a zipped pocket.

4 They should provide deep pockets able to accommodate a cup of juice, toddler wipes, and toys that had to be taken out with you but were discarded at the most inconvenient moment. It is bizarre how much junk is required when out and about with a child. In some ways it is expected with a baby because of nappies, nappy sacks, creams, powder, change of clothes and all the rest of it, but it doesn't go away. It just changes shape to the point where it is a drink, a half eaten sandwich (the other half of which will be required later), a toy, or whatever. There seem to be two choices: the plastic carrier bag or the deep pockets.

5 They must be capable of surviving being washed on a daily basis. The only thing that gets more dirt on it than a small child is the parent.

6 You must not care about whether they get ruined. Part of this relates to point five above, but also to the fact that most children's activities seem to require Dad to spend a large amount of time crawling around the floor, crawling on grass, or otherwise spending time on his knees.

The danger is that your regular wardrobe eventually consists of only three pairs of tracksuit trousers and six sweatshirts. The only reason it is so large is that at any point in time at least two pairs of trousers and four sweatshirts are in the wash. That's when the washing machine runs every day. Stay at home Dad clothes should not, under any circumstances, be fashionable or expensive.

DRESSING UP

After a while, this casual dress does (and this sounds hard to believe) start to become less liberating than one would imagine. The only problem is that there's little incentive to dress up. There is nothing to dress up for. The child doesn't care, and nobody else seems to either. It really doesn't matter what you look like, until eventually you spot yourself in the mirror and see a slightly overweight man with a baby wearing cheap no-brand tracksuit trousers and a faded sweatshirt that has been washed too many times. The first time I saw myself like this it was a shock. I used to look good in a suit and tie with a freshly laundered and pressed white shirt and one of a collection of silk ties.

As a result, anything can now be an excuse to dress up for a short while, and to look like something other than a scruff. Strangely, I have found myself dressing more formally to go to the supermarket, or to attend any of the children's entertainments that do not involve adults cleaning a dusty floor with their clothes. I am the only person I know who puts on a jacket specifically to go to Tesco.

It was also a fabulous initial experience no longer to have to shave every day. Suddenly life was a never ending Sunday morning, but without the newspapers. After some weeks I declared, more out of embarrassment than any real commitment, that I was growing a beard. My wife informed me of a previously unsuspected allergy to facial hair, and that was the end of that. Daily shaving returned, but with the added bonus of a two year old with an elephantine memory who looks at me every morning, and in a concerned tone enquires, "Dad, when are you going to shave?"

PHYSICAL DEMANDS

Office life doesn't provide the best preparation for childcare. (Thinking about it, sitting on my backside for eight hours a day didn't prepare me very well for anything other than sitting on my backside for another eight hours a day.) It has been a genuine surprise to me how physically fit you have to be in order to look after a small child. Every activity involved in childcare seems to require a level of physical capability way in excess of anything I have needed to be able to do on a day to day basis since I parted company with a particularly enthusiastic physical education teacher at secondary school.

For example:

- Even once they can walk, the number of occasions when it is necessary to carry a 30 pound plus two year old is innumerable: escalators, stairs, crossing the road while people rev their engines as if the additional noise will actually encourage a small child to walk faster rather than stop and watch.
- Putting a child in a car seat requires a level of physical flexibility only achieved by years of yoga, or six months looking after a child.
- Carrying shopping, plus a pushchair, plus child, while getting on a train is an act of superhuman strength and dexterity normally only seen in fantasy comic books.
- Putting an unwilling child in a supermarket trolley is a master class in the precise use of gentle strength. It is surprising where a child can get his legs when he doesn't want them to go where you want them to.
- Playing with a small child requires the ability to spend most of your time on your knees. For the first time since I was 12 I have actually worn out a pair of jeans at the knees rather than at the waistline.

And there are thousands more examples of everyday activities designed to test your physical capabilities to the limit. One of the first things I discovered when I started to look after a small child was that I was nowhere near as fit as I thought I was. If I had known half of what I would need to be able to do, I would have spent the whole nine months of pregnancy on an exercise regime to achieve the peak physical condition that is needed to be able to deal with this.

Of course, it is just as well that all this physical activity is required, as there are far more opportunities to put on weight at home than there are in the office. The biscuit tin is always handy, and there are always children's chocolates around the place, and all those half eaten meals need to be finished off by someone.

It is easy to become too casual in your approach to dressing for the day, with the justification that this is the most appropriate way to dress for a day of childcare. The problem arises when this is interpreted as 'letting yourself go' now that you don't have the essential discipline of work. How you dress gives many people an impression of who you are and what your life is like. If you're dressed as a shabby tramp with two kids in tow, who's to say that they're not wrong?

PART 2:
Staying at Home

Introduction

Being at home all day is a very different experience from going to work for the day. The process of going to work in the morning involves a series of small rituals that provide a very clear distinction between home and work. Things that we take for granted, such as the simple tasks of shaving, dressing for work, and travelling to the workplace all help to create space between home life and work life.

For the stay at home Dad there is immense initial pleasure in not shaving, not having to wear a suit, and not leaving the house to join the morning rush to work, but it isn't that long before you could be looking in the mirror one morning to be faced by a slovenly, unshaven, badly dressed man whose looks as if he's about 20 pounds heavier than you are. The mirror does not lie. That is you as you are now. Worse than that, it is you as your children are seeing you. It is the only evidence your family and friends need to be able to start saying "I told you so." Imagine what your partner's thinking.

It's something of a shock to the system when you realise you haven't been further than the front door for three days and you find yourself justifying your appearance as just a result of your voluntary absence from society. Treating life as if it was one long Sunday morning is not what you hoped it would be. It is instead a clear sign that you are losing it.

Meanwhile, your partner is going through her own daily rituals, and leaving the house every morning to get to the office where she spends the day with real adults (who have shaved and dressed) and participating in real life. It would be unnatural if there weren't times when you develop a sense of longing for the days when you were out there too.

WHAT IF YOU JUST CAN'T DO IT?

There is the chance that, despite all the best intentions, being a stay at home Dad is just simply not going to work for you or your situation. A big question that has to be considered when thinking about becoming a stay at home Dad is what you are going to do if this proves to be the case. What is plan B?

When I first became a stay at home Dad, my wife and I had a number of options that we considered. These included:

- Working full time, my wife combining part time work with the primary care role, and using a day nursery the rest of the time.
- Both working part time and sharing the childcare responsibilities.
- Our worst-case scenario was both working full time and using professional childcare on a full time basis.

The option for my wife to become a stay at home Mum wasn't possible for pragmatic financial reasons as well as her desire to continue her career.

Your plan B will obviously depend on your personal circumstances, but it is well worth making sure you have a plan B, regardless of your confidence in never needing to exercise it.

Being at home for seven days a week is very different from being home for the weekend even when children aren't involved. The quiet country lane where I live at the weekend is, during the working week, a semi-official racetrack for insane tractor drivers, and all those nice neighbours you expected to be able to socialise with are out at work.

The house you live in is very different during the week. Being there for seven days a week means you notice more about your home. Everything in the house needs painting, fixing, repairing, or otherwise enhancing now that you have to put up with it every day.

The moment you become a stay at home Dad, there are cracks that appear in the plaster on the walls that simply weren't there before. Cupboard doors stick, taps drip, and floorboards creak. Of course, it's always been like that, but when you had more than enough to do at the weekend, and it wasn't bad enough to get someone in to do it, these things didn't bother you that much. Now that you have to put up with them all week, and on a single income it doesn't make sense to pay someone to fix them, they start to assume a level of importance that is completely out of proportion to the reality of the situation.

Just to add to this your partner (who, let's remember, still sees the house for only two days a week) not only doesn't notice any of these things, she also fails to acknowledge their fundamental importance to life as we know it. In my case, my partner being in the house for just two days a week generated a completely different list of things that needed doing, which she would helpfully write out in block capitals and leave stuck to the fridge (that being the place where she suspected I was likely to spend a significant portion of the day).

This change in perception of your home, combined with the close proximity of the fridge, are both small factors in determining that (and this is ironic) when you give up work to stay at home with the kids, one of the most important things you have got to do is to get out of the house.

SIX BIG REASONS WHY YOU HAVE GOT TO GET OUT OF THE HOUSE

1 If you stay in the house all day you will get very bored.

2 More importantly, if you stay in the house all day the kids will get very bored. A bored stay at home Dad plus bored kids is a guaranteed bad time for all concerned.

3 You're not going to meet anyone (with the possible exception of the postman, and they've got a job to do) by staying at home. The only realistic way to get any adult company is to get out and about.

4 In an age when many of us do not live on the same street as our parents and grandparents, building and maintaining a local support network is essential. This isn't going to happen by watching TV.

5 If you're not out with the kids then what are you going to have to talk to your partner about when she politely asks how your day was? The quality of daytime television is a one time conversation. The more you do during the day, the more enjoyable the rest of the time is.

6 If you don't go out, your life will become one long DIY activity.

Being out of the house provides more stimulation for you and the kids, it makes the day go more quickly, and provides you with the opportunities to build the support network of friends and acquaintances that will prove invaluable to your future success as a stay at home Dad. It also helps to deal with one of the issues faced by all stay at home parents, which is that of feeling isolated now that they are at home with a child.

How you manage the challenges of being at home will go a long way towards determining how successful you are as a stay at home Dad. Having overcome the shock and emotional pain of leaving work and embarking on this new role, a whole new world awaits you. This is a world that is very different to the one you have left behind.

It is a world that you are facing with one salary rather than two, it is a world created for and occupied by women, and a world that seems to be dominated by the needs of children and the daily battle to maintain a household in some kind of state suitable for human habitation. Being a stay at home Dad in this world will change the way you think about yourself, it will change you as a person, and it will change your relationship with your partner. You will discover latent skills you never knew you had, and very quickly learn how to tell the difference between the washing machine and the oven.

Dealing with Isolation

One of the big issues faced by anyone who leaves their job to stay at home with the children is a feeling of isolation. This is not an issue that is specific to stay at home fathers, but as many of the mechanisms for dealing with it are geared towards mothers it is worth thinking about this as a stay at home Dad.

PREVENTION IS BETTER THAN CURE

The only way to deal with isolation is to do whatever you can to prevent it. Most of us do not live within screaming distance of our family, and it is likely that most of our existing friends will still be at work all day. It is therefore essential to build the local friendships and relationships that suit your new role, and which can be a source of support and encouragement when required, and a great resource for practical advice and assistance, as well as tea and sympathy. It is fortunate that children are the world's best way to meet other people, and provide a natural and enjoyable conversation starter, as long as you make the effort and get out of the house.

After a while you will start to become a familiar face at whatever activities or gatherings you choose to attend, and everyone else will start to become familiar faces to you.

BEING THE ONLY MAN IN THE ROOM

There are times when it feels intimidating to be the only man in a room full of young mothers, and it's certainly nothing like the adolescent fantasies that single men may imagine but, incredible as it may sound, the whole process is just as intimidating for a lot of the women involved. There is no gender conspiracy, and while your ability to contribute to conversations concerning breastfeeding, stage two of childbirth, or the physical effects of pregnancy may be limited, you can make just as valid a contribution to the more regular discussions on children's health and development.

It is surprising how quickly the shared experiences are more important than the differences between being a man or a woman at home. You do also have the natural advantage that many of the mothers will be intrigued by what you are doing and why. We all know that nobody has to ask many men more than once to talk about their favourite subject.

TIPS FOR PREVENTING ISOLATION

1 Start thinking about and building a support network before the baby is born if possible.
2 Attend the antenatal classes with your partner. (My experience has been that stay at home mothers have been much easier to become friends with if they have already met my partner, as I mentioned earlier.)
3 Make contact with your local group of the National Childbirth Trust if you have one. They will run regular events and opportunities to meet people in your area.
4 Once the baby is born, attend whatever postnatal groups you can with your partner while she is on maternity leave.

5   Go to the weekly health visitor's clinics for weighing and measuring the baby (whether they need weighing and measuring or not). There is usually a queue and it's a good time to meet people.

6   Find out about any open invitation coffee mornings that are being run for parents and children and go to them.

7   Enrol in local activity classes for babies and pre-schoolers. A huge range is available, covering everything from gymnastics to music.

8   If there is a local play area go there on a regular basis. If you pick the same time and day, it is likely you will start to see the same people there with their children.

9   Look for activities in local sports halls and swimming pools. For example, one morning a week our local sports centre is given over to a range of toys and apparatus for the under fives. After a few weeks, the same familiar faces start to make contact.

THE ATTRACTIONS OF STAYING IN

There are times however when staying in the house all day will seem like an attractive option. It's probably not something you've had the chance to do very much of in the past, it's cold, it's raining, and there's a lot you need to do around the house. Getting out of the house with a couple of small children is also a major activity in its own right, requiring a full scale logistical operation and perfect timing. There is no such thing as a quick trip out any more. Just to get out of the house used to take me an average of 40 minutes.

With my two children the process of getting to the point of leaving the house involves:

• Changing the baby's nappy as a fresh nappy tends to do better than an old one if there is anything to deal with while out.

• Changing the baby into some decent clothes so nobody will think

I'm not trying. (Hint: never take a small baby out in a sleep suit. It looks like you've not changed them from the night before and can lead to much pursing of lips.)

- Making sure the changing bag contains sufficient numbers of nappies, nappy sacks, wipes, clothes, sun cream, hats, and who knows what else.
- Getting sufficient milk into the cool bag to last for the whole trip.
- Cramming the fabulously expensive but completely unusable travel system (the new word for pram) into the boot of the car, despite the fact it is designed only to fit into a small truck.
- Placing small child in car seat and getting the seat into the car.
- Getting toddler into clothes suitable for outside, putting on shoes.
- Convincing toddler that the car seat is not a monster and is safe to sit in.
- Taking toddler to the toilet before going.

All this just to go to the supermarket, and in the certain knowledge that both of the children will fall asleep in the car and will need to be woken when we get there in 15 minutes, thus disrupting their nap routine and leading to two crabby children for the rest of the day. They looked so happy just sitting in the front room, it seems a shame to disturb them.

Staying in the house is not an option however, and the feelings of isolation can be very real for stay at home Dads and for mothers who stay at home as well. After spending the majority of your adult life being out every day, going to work, meeting people, and being in a social environment, taking on the life of a parental hermit is not an easy adjustment. Despite the attractions of staying in, it is essential to get out, meet people, and build a local support network that will stand you in good stead for the future. It is also important to remember that this isn't just about you; there are the children to consider as well. They need to be out and about as much, if not more than you do.

Getting Organised

Essential to your success will be your ability to get organised. Basic childcare tasks need to be organised and planned. Anyone who has had a hungry baby overnight and no bottles made will know that being organised enough to have the bottles ready is far preferable to the noisy alternative. It is important to plan activities for the children, and to be organised enough to be able to fit in the housework at the same time.

A LONG TERM PLAN

As well as being organised on a day to day basis it is also important to have a long term plan for what you are doing, and how your role as a stay at home Dad fits into that plan. There aren't any right or wrong answers as to what this plan should look like, but it should address some key questions about how you are going to approach the role. For example:

a   Are you a full time stay at home Dad, to the exclusion of all other activities, or is there the possibility of part time work?

b   Do you intend to return to work when the children go to school?

c   Do you intend to re-enter your previous profession at some point? (Some stay at home fathers are lucky enough to be offered the option of a career break, but this is the exception rather than the rule.)

d   Is being a stay at home Dad an opportunity to acquire new skills and experience to enable you to change your career direction?

e Is it an opportunity to do something completely different or entrepreneurial while also looking after the kids?

How you decide to approach your time as a stay at home Dad will go a long way to determining what you get out of it, and will determine what you do while being a stay at home Dad. For example, if your plan is to return to your current profession, then you need to maintain skills and contacts throughout your absence in order to ease your re-entry to the workplace.

Some general rules while devising the plan however are:

a Do not overestimate how much time will be available outside your childcare role. That cute little baby who naps for three hours a day will soon turn into a demanding and time consuming toddler who doesn't sleep though the night yet, let alone during the day. You will also have plenty of other things to keep you occupied. Realistically, you will have very little spare time, if any.

b Do not imagine that your ex-colleagues will be spending their time waiting excitedly for your return to work. Life goes on, with or without you.

c It is incredibly difficult to plan on anything when children are involved. The one time you need them to nap in the afternoon will be the one time they don't. For the stay at home Dad the kids are the primary responsibility and everything else has to take second place.

d It is quite possible that you will be more exhausted than you have ever been before. Your enthusiasm for that self-study course may well not be at its highest at nine o'clock in the evening when the kids have finally gone to sleep.

A sense of realism is essential. If your job is to look after the kids then that is what comes first. The rest of it is secondary. It might be important to you, but it is definitely secondary.

WEEKLY PLANS

Without wanting to turn an enjoyable childcare experience into some kind of project, I have found that short term plans are also important. It is very easy to spend all day looking after the children, and then for all day to turn into all week, and all week turn into all month, without ever getting a sense of achieving anything other than just getting through the days. It's important to avoid that 'where did the day go?' feeling.

THE WEEKLY PLAN

A plan doesn't have to be particularly complicated, but the example of a weekly plan below does help to:

1 Show where there are areas of the week when there is nothing to do. Sitting around the house isn't good for anyone.
2 Enable you to prepare for the day.
3 Record what it is you actually did.

	Morning	Afternoon
Monday	Gymnastics Class	Household chores
Tuesday	Music Class	Library
Wednesday	Friend's house for coffee	Household chores
Thursday	Shopping	Trip to the park
Friday	NCT Coffee Morning	

This plan was for a toddler aged two. He regularly napped in the afternoon, which meant that chores could be more easily completed without his help. Although the classes he attended were only one hour long, by the time we were ready to go, got there and got home again, that was pretty much the morning dealt with.

The plan is not particularly detailed, but it did help to achieve the following:

1   It enabled me to know what I was planning to do in advance so that I could prepare for it.
2   Every day included something that forced getting out of the house.
3   It included time interacting with other children.
4   It included time interacting with other adults.
5   It provided the basis for knowing where the days went.

By approaching being a stay at home father in an organised way, you can avoid a lot of problems that result from being unorganised. By using a plan you can be very clear about:

1   Why you are being a stay at home father.
2   What you are planning to do as a stay at home father.
3   When you are planning to do it.

However, there does need to be a health warning attached to any plan regarding children. One of the key attributes that all experienced stay at home Dads seem to recognise is the ability to be flexible and adapt. Children are something of a loose gun on deck and can very quickly turn any plan into wishful thinking regardless of how much time, effort, and forethought Dad has put into it.

Finances

In most cases, becoming a stay at home Dad means going from two incomes to one, while at the same time experiencing a huge increase in costs because of the arrival of your bundle of joy. This is a fairly impressive double whammy. This is no different to many cases when the mother stays home, of course. However, as well as being aware of the reduced income and the obvious costs of having children, it is also important to be aware of the almost limitless opportunities for spending money that are provided by being a stay at home Dad.

THE COSTS OF A CHILD

The initial major additional costs are those that are associated with the fact of having a child. Children are not cheap. If you just want something to look after get a cat. They are less expensive and tend to be quieter.

The average cost of raising a child to the age of 21 in the UK is estimated at £140,000 and change.[5] And that assumes you educate them in the state system. That is an astounding £6,686 every year, or more than £500 a month – for 21 years. Kids or Ferraris, you pay your money and you take your choice.

---

5 Source: Liverpool Victoria Friendly Society Press Release, 21st November 2003.

BREAKDOWN OF COSTS OF A CHILD BY AGE

Years 1 – 5	£46,695
Years 6 – 11	£31,000
Years 12 – 18	£33,747
Years 19 – 21	£30,000[6]

Of the above costs, the first year alone is estimated to cost more than £7,000. All of this is interesting (and frightening) but relevant as a warning that you need to be aware of the financial impact.

Children seem to cost as much as you have got to spend on them (like work expanding to fill the time available), and if you waited to have children until you were sure you could afford them, then you'd still be waiting. The best advice at this point is to forget any false pride and take whatever free gifts, hand-me-downs or grandma's knitting, that you can get your hands on.

DAILY COST INCREASES

In addition to the costs of now being a parent, a whole range of additional costs and expenses start to become apparent on a daily basis.

The first area where additional expense will occur is just through the very process of there now being someone in the house all day. Heat and light are not unjustifiable luxuries, but they do cost more money than when both of you were out of the house all day. Electricity, gas, water, telephone: all of the utility bills will increase as the house is being used more. This isn't only as a result of Dad being at home, but is also a natural consequence of having a baby in the house. Dad might be able to put on a sweater and be cold for a bit, but it's unlikely that the baby is going to take to it. (Actually Dad's probably not going to put up with it for long either.) There seems to be no way round this, except to use your time to ensure you get the best possible deal on the utilities from different suppliers.

The second area where it is easy to spend more money is on entertainment for the kids. Sadly, nobody is providing indoor play areas, music classes, or toddler gymnastics as a philanthropic gesture. They all cost money, and although on their own none of them appears to be outrageously expensive, they all add up.

Thirdly, there are the 'but I just couldn't resist it' purchases. Although you wouldn't notice it until you went out with a small child, every shelf in every shop is stacked from floor to ceiling with the very thing that would be just perfect for your particular child.

I suspect that because fathers are presented with a very specific image of the role of the father (based on a traditional weekend participation in family life) we find it particularly difficult to resist indulging in the role of the bountiful provider when we are out with our children. When the opportunity to be the generous father arises on a daily basis rather than just at the weekend, then this can become a problem. A heart of stone may not seem like the ideal characteristic to qualify you for being a stay at home Dad but there are, sadly, times when it is an essential part of your character. I have found it useful to remember that any purchase will require explaining to my wife when she gets home from work, earning the money that I have just spent.

The fourth potential for spending money is when it is the child and not the father who decides that the goods on display are just what is required to make their life complete. This is the curse of pester

6 Source: ibid.

power. As fathers we are a soft touch for those big blue eyes and the plaintive "Pleeeeeeease." The heart of stone is required once again. At the checkout, walking up the aisles, and even outside a shop window, pester power seems to be able to strike at any time, and from a surprisingly early age. Before they can even talk, they will cry when they see something they want in a shop window.

It is all too easy to give in, not only because you want a bit of peace and quiet (God knows you've earned it, and it's only 50 pence after all) but also because you want to see the happy smiling face of your child looking up at their wonderful father. It's a cheap thrill. Resisting this temptation is an ongoing battle, but it is one that has to be won. It will not be long before it's a car for their seventeenth birthday. The only way to win the fight against pester power is by setting the right expectation, and establishing the precedents that you are prepared to live with. I have found it useful to remember that cars are expensive.

DON'T MAKE PESTER POWER WORSE

Every action you take with a small child seems to set a precedent. It sets a precedent for them, and it also sets a precedent in your own mind as to what behaviour you have decided is acceptable. Unless you want to buy chocolate every time you go into the supermarket don't make a big thing about doing it the first time, or every trip to the supermarket from then on will end in trauma for all concerned.

Of course it's great fun to have a little treat while you're out with the kids. As a general rule, fathers again seem to be more susceptible to this than mothers. Unfortunately, every treat sets an expectation. Soon it isn't a treat any longer. Exceptions to the rule are the rule. Kids seem to remember the treat, but they are very adept at forgetting the specific context in which the treat was given. It is now the standard for behaviour. My own particular downfall has been the pick and mix at the supermarket. Every trip to the store is now a race to get to the last aisle where the offending items are stocked, and where I foolishly introduced my toddler to the delights of strawberry fondant. Every time you do anything as a treat it is essential to remember that you are establishing a precedent and setting an expectation for the future.

The fifth way in which the opportunity to spend money arises is through the essential supermarket shopping. Supermarkets do not make their profits without knowing how to take money off you. They are exceptionally good at this. I have started to look at every trip to the supermarket as a battle of wills that I have got to win. Their objective from my trip to the supermarket is for me to spend as much time and as much money as possible while I am there, but without finding everything I need to buy, thus necessitating a return visit to buy those items I failed to purchase on this trip. My objective is to get in and out of the store in the minimum amount of time, spending the minimum amount of money, and leaving with everything I need for the week.

It is important to remember that the supermarket's objectives are not my objectives. The supermarket wants me to think of it as if it is my friend, but actually it just wants to take my money off me as often as possible.

When I first started doing the weekly shopping for our family I was constantly forgetting things and needing to return to the store later in the week. As a result, our shopping bill went up by more than 20 per cent. Mine is not a unique experience.

KEEPING THE SHOPPING BILL UNDER CONTROL

1   Only go there once a week. It is very difficult to go to a supermarket and only come out with what you went in there for. After all, you've made the effort to get the kids out and go there, which is a lot just for a pint of milk, and oh look, chocolate doughnuts are on special offer today, and you're pretty sure that you're short of cereal, and well now you're here you might as well get a few things. If every time you need a pint of milk it leads to a £10 shopping trip then the supermarkets are winning.

2   Make a list and stick to it. Making a list achieves two key things. Firstly it should stop you from buying all those good things that you neither need nor really want, but that the supermarkets want to sell you. Secondly, it's a lot more fun to have the 'shall we buy?' conversation with your partner while constructing a shopping list, than it is to have the 'why the hell did you buy?' conversation with her when she discovers what's in the cupboard.

3   Learn the layout of the store. By knowing the layout of the store you can construct a shopping list that matches your path through the supermarket. This can speed up your overall trip through the store, as well as reducing the number of temptations you meet on your way round. Of course, every now and then the store will change where they keep everything, which is thoroughly annoying, and one suspects is done for the express purpose of making you wander round the store looking for things you buy every week, in the hope that you will find previously undiscovered delights that you will not be able to live without. There doesn't seem to be much you can do about this except complain to anyone who will listen, and that's not going to change anything.

4   Watch the 'sell by' dates. The 'sell by' and 'use by' dates are pathetically close together on a lot of products. Bizarrely this particularly seems

to be the case on items that can only be bought as multi-packs. However hard you try to make them, no kid is going to eat 12 fromage frais in two days. When I first started shopping we ended up throwing a lot of stuff away. Unfortunately, just because you throw it away doesn't mean it was any cheaper.

5   Check the bill. It is always worth checking the bill and complaining. Sometimes you will get an apology payment as well as the correction. This particularly applies to multi-savers where the tills sometimes don't recognise the offers that are displayed on the shelves. It doesn't seem to happen very often, but it's free money.

6   Take the kids. With the availability of 24 hour shopping it is often tempting to sacrifice an evening and have a long leisurely stroll round the store without any interruptions or distractions. This temptation should be resisted for three reasons.

   a   Taking the kids will encourage a more hasty trip round the store and should reduce the temptation to spend more.

   b   A trip to the store is, in the early years, as good an outing as anything for the kids.

   c   You should make sure you have better things to do in the evenings when the kids are asleep than go to the supermarket.

FROM TWO INCOMES TO ONE

As well as increased costs, whether it is Mum or Dad who is staying at home there is normally no way around the fact that two incomes will reduce to one. This is not unique to the situation where it is Dad who stays home, but given that money can be a major source of stress in any relationship (or rather, the lack of money can be a major source of stress in any relationship) it is worth giving this special attention when Dad stays home because it is Dad who is traditionally meant to be the provider.

However much your partner accepts what you have decided to do, and however much you intellectually believe that this is the best way to structure your family roles and responsibilities, there will come a time when you will tell yourself that you are the one who should be out there earning. If money is tight then it is likely that you are going to tell yourself this more frequently and with increasing bitterness as time goes by. The funny thing is that this thought probably hasn't even crossed your partner's mind.

The reduction in income as a result of going from two salaries to one means that it is normally necessary to get more serious about money as a stay at home Dad. Financial issues can cause stress in any relationship, and being a stay at home father does not mean that yours will be immune from this. However, being at home does give the opportunity to do more management of home finances than may have been either necessary or possible when both partners were working full time.

Specific actions that can help include:

• Doing a monthly budget and sticking to it. Budgeting for expenses not only lets you know where you intend to spend money, but also highlights where you spent money that you did not intend. Of course, one way to budget would be for your partner to give you a weekly housekeeping allowance, but there are no indications that this approach has proved acceptable in any stay at home Dad household, and most are operating from a joint bank account rather than from carefully divided wage packets.

• Tracking expenditure so that you know where the money actually goes – especially if you have a habit of using cash, as when you're not locked in the office all day it is amazing how often you have to go to the cash point. (A cup of coffee here, a magazine there, a newspaper, some sweets for the kids, admission to the play area, now where is that 50 quid I took out this morning?)

- Use your spare time to save money by stopping all the things that waste money, but just weren't that important when you were both bringing in a salary. This includes making sure you're on the right phone package for your family, getting the best electricity and gas deal that you can, shopping for the best insurance, and cancelling all those movie subscriptions on the television because you're not going to have time anyway.

- You can, if you are that way inclined, start mending and fixing things, growing vegetables, building the kids toys from discarded pallets. How much money this saves is debatable, but taking a broken washing machine apart can provide a great project to undertake with a toddler.

You also need to consider pension plans. In particular there is a danger of risking a large gap in the record of your contributions for a state pension if you do not get the paperwork sorted on this. You must ensure that you are registered as the main payee for child benefit in order to qualify for Home Responsibilities Protection on your pension contributions.[7] There is also a decision to make as to whether to continue with contributions to a personal pension plan. At a time when money is inevitably in shorter supply than it has been it is tempting but not necessarily sensible to put this off.

MATERNITY LEAVE

One other aspect of becoming a stay at home Dad that can have a sig-

---

7 More information available from leaflets provided by The Pensions Service and available at www.pensionguide.gov.uk.

nificant financial impact is if you and your partner choose to have more children. When Dad has given up work to look after the kids and then you have another child the two incomes have not just reduced to one, they have reduced to none. (You can't count statutory maternity pay as an income, believe me.) When it is Mum who is at home anyway, there is no question of her taking six months leave from looking after the other kids in order to go on maternity leave, although I am sure it sounds like a nice idea. When it is Mum who is going into the office every day, there may be no option but for her to take an extended period of time off as maternity leave. Suddenly two incomes are no incomes. There are no ways around this. In terms of minimising the impact, the only possibilities seem to be:

- For your partner to reduce the length of maternity leave to the minimum practical.

- To plan for the additional child and save enough money to be able to cover all expenses for an extended maternity leave. (Of course, you may not have planned having a new baby when you were 87, but medical science can do the strangest things.)

- Stop being a stay at home Dad on a temporary basis and get a job on a short term contract for the period of maternity leave.

None of these options may be either reasonable or practical. Reducing maternity leave to the minimum may be neither emotionally nor physically sensible. Saving to cover several months of no income may not be possible, given that you have already reduced from two incomes to one. Dad suddenly disappearing off to work when the new baby arrives may not seem like the right thing to do from the point of view of you, your partner or your children. The only good news here is that this is the only serious, full scale, unfixable major disadvantage I have found to being a stay at home Dad.

There is no escaping the financial issues associated with becoming a stay at home Dad. The initial costs of parenthood are significant. For a start there are high chairs, pushchairs, bath chairs, and bouncy chairs. It is bizarre how many chairs one child seems to need. Cots, prams, toys, clothes, changing mats and baby baths. The list is almost endless. Added to this, a proportion of the family income has just disappeared as Dad has given up work. It suddenly becomes important to watch where the money is being spent, plan a budget, and find ways to minimise the outgoings. For Dad in particular it is important to avoid giving the impression of profligacy. It is much too easy to spend money when you're not in the office all day.

Working Part Time

One way in which some of the financial issues of giving up an income and having children could be alleviated is if you can combine childcare with working part time, or working from home. This may not strike you as fair, but get used to it, plenty of stay at home Mums do. However, it is not that easy. Combining childcare and working part time is nothing like it is portrayed in the movies. The dashing executive making deals with a baby in his arms has no basis in reality. It is likely to be a bad deal and an unhappy baby, as he would not have been concentrating fully on either of them.

The idea that working part time should be easy is also encouraged by the number of high profile parents who continue to follow their exotic careers while caring for their children. While I have no doubt that they must find parenthood as big a change as the rest of us, the three nannies, two personal tutors, driver, and assorted maids and bodyguards must help I guess. Unless you are very fortunate, it is unlikely that all these advantages will be available to you. You and your partner will have to find a way to manage it on your own.

Despite what seems like never ending publicity regarding family friendly working policies and the importance that is placed on the role of the father in the family, there are very few part time jobs available that fit around the demands of looking after the children. You could put them into day care of course, but then why did you decide to be a stay at home father in the first place? Day care isn't always the answer anyway.

PART TIME JOBS

Most part time jobs that would allow you to carry on caring for the children may represent a significant downsize in both salary and responsibility from what you are used to. If your partner is in a normal nine to five role, and she is able to take over the childcare outside those times, then your options are limited to jobs that can be done in the evenings and at weekends. Some stay at home mothers do find a way to combine earning and childcare by becoming a childminder in addition to looking after their own children. I have yet to find a stay at home father who has taken this approach to earning. Our own children tend to be enough to keep us busy.

When you first left work it is possible that there were promises of some ad hoc consultancy work, or perhaps some project work that could be done from home that would help with the inevitable reduction in income. However well meant these promises were at the time, they are unlikely to represent a reliable source of future earnings. If any of the promises come to anything, consider it a bonus. If, after two years, anyone at the office remembers who you were, consider it a miracle.

COMBINING WORK AND CHILDCARE

When you first take on childcare responsibilities you may also have an unrealistic expectation of what can be achieved by combining childcare and part time work. The small baby you agreed to take care of was having two naps a day for two hours a time. You could get a full day's work in during that time with no distractions if you really put your mind to it. Unfortunately there is plenty that has to be done while the child is asleep, including washing, cooking, cleaning and otherwise managing the home, and catching up on the sleep you're not getting overnight. Those four hours are important for other reasons than trying to cram a full day's work into them, and the only thing that can be guaranteed about a baby's nap time is that the first time you really need them to nap because you have a deadline to make or someone to meet, they won't. Not only will they not nap, they will scream for the whole time you were supposed to be working. This period of long naps doesn't last long anyway, and soon that amenable child who entertained himself quite happily with a home made sock puppet becomes a demanding toddler who needs constant attention or he will burn the house down.

After a few years, as pre-school options become available, there is more potential for part time work, but it still has to be something that can be fitted around the demands of both the children and your partner's job. Through all of this it is important to remember that whatever part time work you do is likely to be nowhere near as important or lucrative as the full time primary earning occupation that your partner has.

BENEFITS OF WORKING PART TIME

There are several benefits to working part time in addition to the obvious one of the money. These include:

1 Maintaining skills in preparation for a return to full time work.
2 Maintaining contacts in preparation for a return to full time work.
3 Providing mental stimulation.
4 Providing adult contact.
5 Keeping you in the habit of working.

PROFESSIONAL CHILDCARE

Even if you make the decision to work part time and use a proportion of your earnings to pay for professional childcare to cover the times when you are working, the position of being the primary carer does not make this as simple as you may expect.

The first problem can often be finding a place for your children in a day nursery or other childcare facility, especially one that is conveniently located. If work involves travelling, hours other than nine to five, or being away overnight, it can be very problematic when children have to be dropped off and picked up.

The hours of most daycare facilities seem to operate around eight to six, and although this seems reasonable enough, there are a number of factors that can make these hours difficult. Firstly, there is the process of dropping off the child. Getting a child into the day nursery is not often a five minute task. Just getting them out of the door can take 15 minutes once shoes have been extracted from the oven, favourite toys have been taken from the child's hands and the screaming has abated to a level where you are prepared to be seen in public.

By the time you get to the nursery it is not normally a case of just leaving them at the door while you make your way to work in a professional manner. The plaintive cries of "Daddy don't go. Stay with me", guarantee that even the toughest of fathers will want to stay behind to ensure their children are settled. This has the added side effect of putting you in exactly the wrong frame of mind for a day at work, and questioning whether you really need to be working in the first place. By starting the process at 8.00 sharp, with a bit of commuting time, it is just about possible to get to work for 9.00. As long as you leave work by 5.30 you can probably be at the nursery before you incur punitive charges for being late (£10 or more for every 10 minutes is not unheard of). You then have the pleasure of picking up your child standing alone and forlorn by the entrance clutching the painting they made for Dad. And this is when things are going to plan.

Just to make things more interesting, children don't normally adhere to the plan. In particular, they don't stick to the plan when they are sick. Ironically, once they go into any form of daycare where they mix with other children they seem to get sick a lot. The absence of a fully developed immune system is something of a disadvantage. Our daycare institution will exclude a sick child, not only for the period of the illness, but for the subsequent 48 hours as well. If you are working part time for one or two days a week, this can easily mean that the whole working week is wiped out by any illness. Why any employer would want to put up with this uncertainty in an employee is beyond me.

The good news is that as they get older this improves beyond measure, but in the early years, it feels as if there is a constant stream of illnesses and absences from daycare. For a long time it felt as if I was spending all my time with my son trying to help him recover from whatever illness he had contracted that week at his day nursery. Of course, even though your child has been excluded, and you have been unable to go to work, you still have to pay for your child's place regardless of whether they were there, and whether you were able to earn the money to pay for it.

It is also difficult to be able to share this problem with your partner. Having reduced to one income it doesn't seem sensible to impact your partner's reputation at work by trying to share the load of sick children, however much they may want to help. You have to face the fact that your part time job is almost certainly not generating as much or as regular an income as your partner's full time career. To put it bluntly, it is simply not as important, and will always have to take third place behind your responsibilities for childcare and your responsibility to support your partner in her career. This is a big change for most stay at home Dads who are used to having a career that is on a par with their partner's.

When I first took on the role of being a stay at home Dad I believed I could continue to work part time, with our first child going into daycare for part of the week. This entailed working as a self-employed training instructor, and was inflexible in hours (as the students would be in class between 9.00 and 5.00 it was, not unreasonably, expected that the instructor would be as well) and obviously required me to be in the classroom on the days I was supposed to be. As a naïve childless man I had imagined being able to get up early and do any preparatory work, drop my son off at nursery and make it to the classroom in time to be able to have a relaxed cup of coffee before the training session started. Putting this plan into practice resulted in a somewhat different experience. A not atypical two days trying to work would go something like:

Day 1 – During the night our small child wakes at 10 pm, 1 am and 3 am. At 5.30 he thinks it is time to get up for the day and demands to be taken to daycare immediately. It is patiently explained to him that the nursery isn't open. Any thought of preparing for the day is now redundant. He falls asleep at 7.45, just as I have asked him to find his shoes. I deliver him, shoeless and asleep, to nursery at 8.20. I make it to work just in time. Picking him up at 10 to six I am informed that he has had "two strange poos." Normally I would have taken this as a sign of natural concern for the well-being of one of their charges, but that was before I was aware of the 'three strange poos and you're out' rule; the assumption being that three strange poos and a child must be sick. Fortunately I am not due to be teaching the following day, but I have a meeting with a potential client that I cannot afford to miss.

Day 2 – The meeting is at 2.00 so I decide to delay my son's arrival at nursery to the last possible moment in order to avoid being telephoned and asked to pick him up the moment he has a bowel movement. Once again, any thought of preparation for the day is just a distant memory.

At 1.00 I risk taking him to nursery wearing my suit for the meeting. As we arrive I notice a distinct and immediately recognisable odour. I change him in the car park, somehow getting him to lie on his back in the boot of the car with his legs sticking out of the back. I have a sudden realisation that none of this was covered in the parenting classes that I attended. As he tries to sit up he bangs his head on the emergency triangle attached to the boot lid, leaving a small gash on his forehead. I deliver him to nursery clean, but with blood seeping from an open wound. I suffer an overwhelming feeling of self-loathing as I realise I am relieved that profuse bleeding isn't sufficient for the nursery to make me take him home.

I get to the meeting on time with the faint smell of nappy sack clinging to me. The potential client is good enough not to mention it, but for some reason my complete lack of preparation seems enough to convince him not to give me the job. Guilt gets the better of me on the way home and I pick my son up at 4.30 rather than doing some work before getting him later.

Working part time gets easier as the children get more settled and as they develop the capability to resist at least some illnesses, but the types of daycare that are affordable to most of us in no way represent a worry free or completely reliable option for working, even on a part time basis.

However, many stay at home Dads do manage to work part time

either with daycare support, or in the evenings and weekends. The benefits of working part time, for financial reasons, for maintaining skills and contacts, and for the satisfaction of working, can be more than sufficient to warrant dealing with the difficulties involved.

Primary Care of the Children

From birth, kids seem to possess a degree of low cunning that is both surprising and in some ways frightening, especially as they seem to develop the capability to use it just before they get teeth. They can't walk, they can't talk, but they can wrap at least one parent round their little finger, and they know how to play one parent off against the other, especially when both parents are closely involved in their care. They know that if one parent has put them to bed, then once they have screamed long enough, the other one will come and get them back out again.

Managing the childcare process (and ensuring consistency in the messages that are given to the children) is one of the many challenges of being a stay at home Dad that are shared by the working partner. It is inevitably difficult for a working mother to give up the almost total control over childcare decisions that seems to be a maternal right. Meal times, bed times, acceptable foods, television, friends, reading material, sweets, bath time, and almost anything else, represent possible areas where any child can exploit a difference of opinion or a different approach from parents.

ROLE REVERSAL

While this isn't unique to the situation where the primary care is being provided by the father, there are some aspects of a stay at home Dad household that can exacerbate it, in particular the expectations of the role of the mother and father that we all have. This will include Dad's desire still to be the fun and interesting weekend and evening entertainer, using his occasional involvement in childcare as a source of treats and excitement, and the expectations that Mum will be the one who will add the day to day discipline, impose teeth cleaning routines and generally adhere to the traditional maternal role that most mothers anticipate, and is expected of them by everyone else.

When you choose to become a stay at home Dad you are taking on the responsibility as the primary care provider for your children. You will be the one who is spending the most time with them, and providing most of the care for them day to day. As a result of this it isn't possible for Dad to carry on as if he was a working father. A treat is not a treat when the child is getting it all the time. It is also not possible for Mum to be the provider of all the structure and discipline that would normally be available. Dad has got to subjugate any irresponsible urges and fulfil the aspects of the primary care role that do not involve playing happily with completely inappropriate toys.

The role of a stay at home Dad remains an unusual situation for a man and, just as importantly, being the partner of a stay at home Dad is an unusual situation for a woman. The default situation is for Mum to stay at home and for Dad to go to work, and when it is Mum who is at home, there isn't normally any reason to raise any questions about who would have the lead role in any decisions regarding the children. Both have got to adapt to a different situation.

When it is Dad who stays at home, it seems natural that Mum would still want a level of involvement probably in excess of the traditional father role, and this is true in many stay at home Dad households. In particular, the working mothers have a very high level of involvement in the evenings and at the weekend. This is by choice and is normally eagerly anticipated by Mum, Dad, and the children. For the stay at home Dad this effectively provides a break from childcare duties (although without exception stay at home fathers seem to remain heavily involved at these times.)

CRITERIA FOR CHILDCARE DECISIONS

As with most aspects of childcare, the best way to define your role in relation to the key decisions seems to be whichever way best suits you, your partner and your children. There is no straightforward right or wrong answer as to who should be involved in what decision and who should have the final say. However you should set some basic criteria, such as:

- Both you and your partner should be happy with the arrangement. There is no point deciding that because it is Dad who stays home he should make all the childcare decisions, if that means that Mum feels excluded from their upbringing.
- The arrangement should be the one that you think is best for the children, and should be consistent for them. If Dad's the boss from Monday to Friday, it is difficult to adjust to Mum being the boss on Saturday and Sunday. (Note: it's not only difficult for the children, it can be difficult for Dad as well.)
- Any arrangement should minimise the need for intense discussion between Mum and Dad.

One specific issue for the stay at home Dad can be the feeling that the responsibility for childcare has just been delegated to you because your partner cannot be there. So (and this can apply to housework as well as childcare) you are only doing the tasks as directed by your partner, to her criteria and standards. Any variation from the guidelines that have been provided will be treated with the utmost suspicion. If this is the case, it can be accompanied by a situation in which Mum takes over the childcare at every opportunity in the evenings and the weekends. This is not, to my mind, a sustainable situation, as it leaves Dad with a role of performing manual chores set down by someone else, and leaves Mum exhausted. This is different from what seems to be the more common situation which is where the primary care role is shared at various times.

PRIMARY CARE STYLES

In general terms, there seem to be four main primary care systems in stay at home Dad households.

1 *Dad's The Boss*

    In this scenario Dad is always the primary care provider for the children. This applies when Mum is at work and also when she is at home, and represents an inversion of the traditional stay at home mother role.

2 *Split Care*

    In this scenario Dad provides the primary care when Mum is not available, doing things his way, but at all other times Mum takes primary care responsibility and does things her way.

3 *Mum's the Boss*

    This scenario is where Dad provides primary care for the children when Mum is working, but only on a delegated basis, and on the strict understanding that the care is being provided in accordance with the rules laid down by Mum.

4 *Shared Care*

    This is the most common scenario (and, I believe, the most satisfying for all concerned) in stay at home Dad households, where Mum and Dad reach joint decisions on the key parenting issues.

It is in effect irrelevant which one is implementing them, as the care would be consistent regardless of whether it is Mum or Dad. In these situations, childcare tasks tend to be shared when both Mum and Dad are available, although there is often a much stronger involvement of the mother in the evenings and at the weekend.

Although it is important to adopt the approach that is best for your specific situation, each approach carries with it some advantages and disadvantages. Most importantly, both the 'Mum's the Boss' and 'Dad's the Boss' approaches effectively exclude or constrain the potential for the other partner to contribute to the primary care responsibilities and to be fully involved in bringing up the children.

Split childcare responsibility brings with it problems of consistency and the potential for heated discussions over whose parenting skills have created the poor behaviour traits that even the most wonderful children exhibit from time to time.

Shared childcare needs a much stronger partnership approach to the role of both being a stay at home Dad and being a working mother. While this may be the most satisfying approach overall, it does need the time and effort to be put into the role up front. However, if you weren't going to put that time and effort in, you probably wouldn't be a stay at home Dad in the first place.

Regardless of the style of primary care that you adopt, being part of a household in which primary care is provided by a stay at home Dad can be difficult for Mum. There is the obvious feeling of missing out on seeing the children grow up, and not being there for many of the important events of the early years. It can also be difficult when the children bond strongly with their father, which may inadvertently give the impression of excluding the mother from the relationship in some way. It can be particularly upsetting when a crying child can only be comforted by Dad, and won't go to their mother.

WHEN MUM TAKES OVER

An indication of how difficult it is for many Mums to give up the primary care role is the fact that most of them do effectively take the lead role on childcare issues when that is possible. This is normally limited to evenings, weekends and vacations, but can also include extended periods of time such as maternity leave, should you have more children.

Although it obviously depends on how long a period of maternity leave your partner takes, I found it ironic that during the tiring first few weeks of having a new baby, when it is generally accepted that fathers need to step up and take more responsibility, as a stay at home Dad this was the time when I was least able to do even what I normally did as a father. Our first child was so pleased to have Mum at home, and there wasn't that much I could do for the second in the first few days. I was just becoming comfortable with feeling completely redundant when fortunately my wife returned to work. As a by-product of my wife's involvement during maternity leave I have also had the time to write this book. That's how redundant I was.

It is interesting that in the long term, many stay at home Dads expect to relinquish the primary care responsibility at some point (normally when the children go to school and both parents are working full time) and the stay at home Dad household will return to a more traditional family model, or an increasingly shared approach at all times. This seems to be a reflection of the pragmatic basis of most stay at home Dad situations where the decision to become a stay at home Dad was a financially driven practical one. It may also be an acknowledgment that the level of care required for older children becomes one of guidance and help rather than a 24 hour day of nappy changing, feeding, and general maintenance, so shared care by both the parents is more appropriate.

Running the House

So far, I have been unable to come up with a reasonable and compelling argument to convince my partner that she should go to work all day and then come home and do all the household chores. I hate to admit it, but it does seem reasonable that, given that I am at home with the kids all day, I should be the one who is responsible for the day to day running of the household.

BEING A HOUSE HUSBAND

Being a stay at home Dad normally involves also being a 'house husband', although most stay at home fathers do not like that particular name. When Mum stays home to look after the kids, there are not that many Dads who have to come home from the office and then do all the household chores, and if they did, they would not be short of advice from their friends about what they should be doing with that particular relationship.

There does not seem to be any reason why this should be any different when Dad stays at home. We are, unfortunately, just as capable of putting a vacuum cleaner over the carpet as most women, and most men have had some passing acquaintance with housework at some stage in their lives. This is normally when living alone or in some kind of shared accommodation (most often with a bunch of mates) and unfortunately this involved housework of a completely different kind.

You can no longer only do any cleaning at all when a new girlfriend is coming round, or your mother is coming to visit. You have got to do it to a standard agreed with your partner now that there are children in the house, and not to the, almost inevitably, much lower standard that was acceptable to a man living in a shared flat.

It is unlikely that you will be allowed to do every household task that is required. It seems that there are a number of tasks that cannot be trusted to a man. This includes anything that involves hand washing, gentle cycles, or using the iron on any setting other than the hottest. When all you've ever owned are jeans, suits that need dry cleaning, and cotton shirts, it is difficult to come to terms with the plethora of fabrics used in women's clothing, and the fact that a lot of them use dyes that don't stay in the cloth when they have any contact with water, or that need special care. While I can now operate all of the household machinery, it seems I am only capable of operating it at full power. I gather that this is typically male.

WHO DOES WHAT IN A STAY AT HOME DAD HOUSEHOLD?

Almost without exception, in a stay at home Dad household, it is Dad who is responsible for all the major household chores, including washing, ironing, cleaning, and cooking, as well as the care of the children. This shouldn't really be a great surprise as many of the stay at home fathers were already in a relationship where these tasks were likely to be shared between partners as both were working full time. I have not found any instances where the mother had not been working, and then went to work for the first time when the father stopped working.

Exclusions from what Dad does around the house tend to be on the request of the mother rather than due to an unwillingness to perform the task on the part of the father, and tend to include specific tasks, for example, doing the flower garden, ironing work blouses etc. In many cases household tasks continue to be shared, with the working mother being involved at the weekends.

However attractive it may be, there is no evidence of stay at home Dads avoiding the less pleasant household tasks like cleaning the toilets. Even though some mothers seem convinced that this would be the case, there is nothing to support them in this view.

It can be difficult for women to let go of the traditional tasks involved in the running of the house. As you become more proficient at the standard day to day home making tasks, your partner may suddenly discover a whole new range of essential household chores that only she is able to perform, such as making jam, pickling tomatoes, or making curtains from a pair of old bedspreads.

MEETING YOUR PARTNER'S STANDARDS

Household chores are not fundamentally difficult things to do, but they are difficult to do every day, and they are difficult to do to somebody else's standards. The reason they are difficult to do every day is that they are a) boring and b) never ending.

There is (believe me) little excitement to be had from dusting the skirting board, especially when you know that you last dusted it only a week ago, and that it will look as if you had never been near it within 48 hours. In general, it has to be admitted that men tend to have a greater tolerance level than women for mess.

One of the reasons why it is difficult for a stay at home Dad to complete the household chores to the standards demanded by their partner is this (clearly genetic) difference in attitude towards mess. I can quite happily leave an untidy room downstairs when going to bed for the evening, on the completely logical basis that:

1 Nobody is going to be using that room overnight.
2 It's highly unlikely that any friends are going to pop in unexpectedly at 11.30 in the evening. (Note that this danger of someone popping in unexpectedly is in fact the driving force behind a huge amount of housework.)
3 It will only get messy again in the morning.

My wife on the other hand demands that it is all picked up and put away.

Despite the fact that, as a stay at home Dad, you might be responsible for the running of the home, it is best to accept at an early stage that you will probably be running it to guidelines set in stone by your partner. It is important that you meet those standards, for reasons other than the desire for a quiet life. Your home is the environment that your partner sees being provided for her children.

Traditionally this has been seen as the exclusive domain and responsibility of the mother. Even when a stay at home Dad is responsible for running the home, their partner will often still feel a level of responsibility for the environment that the children are living in. This will manifest itself in a variety of ways, including your partner taking over the running of the home at the weekend, and sometimes tasks that you think have been completed satisfactorily being redone. Personally, I have yet to find a way round this. I would love to be able to say that my wife no longer has to participate in any of the household chores, but it is simply not the case. Part of her cannot let go of this. (In some cases it is a lack of trust, particularly in relation to anything made of silk or which needs hand washing. These are what we refer to in our house as 'reserved powers', emphasising the fact that in reality running the house has only been delegated to me, rather than it being a task that is owned by me.)

However, you can best support for your working partner by freeing her as far as possible from the natural maternal worries about the cleanliness of the place where her children are spending their days. Running the home effectively is important for that if for no other reason.

FINDING YOUR OWN APPROACH

Experience suggests that it is important to find an approach to housework that suits your personal style, and minimises the boredom while maximising the effectiveness of what is fundamentally an unpleasant task.

Initially I tried the approach of turning the household chores into a significant event, and challenged myself to find a way to do them better than they had ever been done before. This was a futile attempt to make them more interesting. Instead of whizzing round with the vacuum cleaner in the areas that were most visible, and ineffectively waving a rag in the general direction of the dusty surfaces, I would pick one room a day and literally take it apart. Furniture would be moved, pictures taken down, curtains removed and books taken from their shelves. Everything would then be individually cleaned and polished before the room was carefully reassembled. This didn't last long. It soon became apparent that this was a huge investment of effort for little visible benefit. When my wife came home and didn't even notice that I had vacuumed the carpet my approach to housework changed. It became a daily chore, to be done in as little time as possible.

The problem with the daily chore approach to housework is that there is little to motivate you to get on with it when it needs doing. As a result housework is now done as quickly as possible. When my partner calls to say that she is leaving work, I know that I have something approaching 45 minutes to make it look as if the whole day has been spent maintaining the family home. Everything is done at double quick time as children disappear in a swirl of moving dust, and every piece of domestic machinery is switched on. More power stations are brought online to deal with the unexpected surge in demand for electricity.

By the time she gets home a scene of complete domestic bliss greets her. The whole house is a combination of smells from dinner in the oven, wet washing, and warm ironing. Of course she isn't fooled by any of this, but she seems happy to play along with this particular charade. (At least I don't think she was fooled by any of it and, if she was, I've blown it now.)

Most household chores can be completed quite effectively with a small child in tow. In fact, many of them provide useful entertainment for toddlers. They will happily put washing into the washing machine and try and push the vacuum cleaner around. It's just a shame that they still need supervision, or I would be one step closer to Utopia.

HOUSEHOLD APPLIANCES

Perhaps the biggest frustration I have encountered with the household chores has been the efficiency of the labour saving devices that exist around the home. While I wouldn't want to be going down to the river to wash clothes, or brushing the floors by hand, it is the case that nothing associated with running the home ever seems to work properly. Vacuum cleaners do not pick up everything. Washing machines are incapable of identifying which clothes contain dye that will stain everything else, the iron cannot determine the right heat setting depending on what you have placed on the ironing board, self-clean ovens simply don't, and I am still trying to work out why a dishwasher should need cleaning.

I have to believe that if men did all the housework, all these problems would be fixed. Not only that, but we would be able to get V8 washing machines with metallic paint and alloy dials; vacuum cleaners would be a mass of chrome and black with an engine tone that would scare dirt out of the house, fingertip controls and a reverse gear. Instead, we are faced with a situation where almost all household appliances seem to be inadequate for the task at hand.

My three year old shares my frustration. Sitting in the bath one night he suggested that the clothes and the dishes should all go in the bath with him so they could all be washed at the same time. It's a thought.

The novelty of running the home soon wears off, especially when it seems it isn't that big a deal after all as far as your partner is concerned. When I first became a stay at home Dad, my wife would return from work and would be given a guided tour of everything that had been achieved that day. Like a small child, I can remember being impressed that I had even managed to work out how to use the washing machine all by myself. My wife was less impressed. You have to get used to the fact that running the home really is a thankless task, and it is just part of the job for a stay at home Dad.

Coping Emotionally

There are days when the world sucks. Even when you are a stay at home Dad and you haven't got to put up with all the hassles of work, there are days when the world sucks. I mean it really sucks.

After a night with a teething baby who seems to have developed a complete resistance to any pain killing medication and who hasn't eaten for three days because their gums hurt too much but somehow still manages to produce copious amounts of diarrhoea on an hourly basis, the stay at home Dad has to wave his partner off to work cheerfully in the morning. You already know that today is going to be one of those days when the office seems like an attractive place to be, when the toddler decides that today is the day when a) he will not do anything you ask, and b) it would be fun to repeat everything you say back to you.

In an attempt to get as much attention as possible, as he is resentful of the new baby, he has decided to regress his potty training to the point at which you might as well never have bothered with it in the first place. As you clean the living room carpet for the third time that morning you are gripped by the horrible realisation that this is your life, and your partner will be out of the house for another eight hours, but only as long as her four o'clock meeting doesn't overrun. When that meeting finishes she'll have "just a couple of things to tidy up" before she leaves the office. Eight hours is the minimum. The smell of burning plastic turns out to be the toddler inserting into the toaster a compact disc your partner left on the counter when she went to work. You have a hundred things you need to do, and you have to get the shopping done. The idea of doing this with two children in their current behaviour mode is one that does not appeal.

Wonderful as they are, children are not designed for a stress free existence on the part of their primary carer. You remind yourself that you were once on the high potential list for a major corporation, and your career might have become something you could have been proud of, yet here you are, unable to cope with two small children.

WHEN KIDS GET POORLY

It doesn't even have to be anything that the kids actually do. In the early years they can be just naturally difficult. They have a lot to come to terms with. They get scared and confused by anything from the television news to the old lady who lives down the road; they have to go through teething, a whole range of injections, and they have no immune system worthy of the name. Perfectly normal healthy children seem to spend a lot of time ill. If they're not ill, then they are about to be ill. If they're not about to be ill, then the next time you go out with them they will end up playing with a child who is ill, and then they will be ill as well. This seems to be the natural order of things and is, you will be told, a good thing as it means they are building up an immunity and they won't have as much time off school when they go. This is not a lot of comfort at this point in your life.

The bad news is that when kids get sick they get bad tempered and crabby. Crabby kids are not as much fun as happy kids. Actually they're not much fun at all, especially the times when 'crabby' appears to have become their default state. As soon as they become ill, all the plans for those great days out with Dad suddenly don't seem like such a good idea. The only thing that seems to matter is whether you can get enough fluid in them to stop them becoming dehydrated from all the diarrhoea and vomiting. Sadly, fluid in can mean fluid out, and it feels as if you're one step away from a trip to the A&E room where your small child will need to be hooked up to an intravenous drip just because Dad didn't have the common sense to be able to cope with a simple stomach virus.

As soon as the kids become ill, it is inevitably a particularly virulent virus, and it is only hours before the stay at home Dad is ill as well. (We all know that men suffer from illness much worse than women. We don't have colds we have the flu, and we don't have a tummy bug, we have a major gastric infection.) And to think that you thought you had to handle pressure and stress in your job. In most cases that will feel as if it was nothing when it comes to dealing with the pressures and stresses of your own children on a daily basis.

DELEGATION

At work there was always the chance to share some of the workload, or perhaps even to delegate some of the more unpleasant tasks. At least there was normally someone you could talk to and share your concerns with, or a boss who you could go to for guidance, however unhelpful it turned out to be.

As a stay at home Dad it can feel as if there are no options available to you. It is you versus the world, and the world is winning. There is nobody to delegate anything to, and nobody you would feel comfortable talking to about how you feel or what you are going through. They would only give you an 'I told you so' look and be confirmed in their opinion that a man really can't take on the role of looking after children. The grandparents are in Portugal on a cheap golfing holiday and your partner is preoccupied with her problems at work. These issues can apply just as much to a stay at home Mum as they do to a stay at home Dad, but there is a difference in that the formal support systems that help parents deal with these challenges are more focused on providing support for a mother than a father.

To make things worse, no one around you seems to be having any difficulty dealing with their children. It's just you. The good news is that this is not really the case. Everyone seems to go through similar problems and similar feelings in response to the strains of daily childcare.

The key thing is to find a way to deal with them and to get access to support when you need it. At times, this may well include lying in wait by the front door for your partner to return home so that you can present her with her children.

THE DIFFICULT TIMES

The constant nature of dealing with children, and the toll that sleepless nights and difficult days can take, can lead to a variety of emotions. These may include:

- Low self esteem as a result of not working any more and potentially feeling that you are not making a worthwhile contribution or coping adequately with your role. Most stay at home Dads who experience this say that it is a temporary emotion in the early days and that the feeling dissipates over time.
- Guilt that your partner has to go out to work all day when she may have been equally happy to stay at home and look after the children.
- Resentment that you are the one who had to give up work while your partner happily continues her career as if you had never had children.

- Envy at your partner's ability to get out of the house every day and do real things with grown-up people.
- Uncertainty about whether you've really done the right thing, whether you can cope as a stay at home Dad, and what it is going to do to the children.
- Disappointment that your old employers seem to have been able to cope perfectly well without you since you left, and in fact your replacement at work is busy undoing every good idea you ever had and blaming you for every failure in the company.
- Concern about your future and whether time out of the workplace as a stay at home Dad is going to ruin your career forever. Most mothers have a tough time re-entering the workplace; imagine the interview you're going to go through when they ask you what you've been doing for the last few years.

Note that all the above emotions are accompanied by an intense self-loathing for having any of these feelings in the first place.

While I'm sure that the occasional intense bout of self-pity can be a healthy cathartic experience and good for the soul, some of these emotions are quite probably nothing more than the result of spending too much time on your own with too much time to think and not enough to occupy your mind. However, regardless of cause, and knowing that "just pull yourself together man" is not always the most useful advice, they need to be dealt with and managed.

If you become unhappy as a stay at home Dad then you have to expect that this will not be good for you or your partner, and most definitely not for the children. Children need your full attention, and not a half-hearted going through the motions stay at home Dad who is quietly wishing he was somewhere else doing something different.

HOW DO YOU COPE?

So how do you cope with all this?

WHAT DO STAY AT HOME DADS DO TO COPE EMOTIONALLY?

1 Get some time for themselves in the evenings or at the weekend.
2 Find a friend they can dump on when necessary.
3 Have a range of people who can take the kids for an hour if needed.
4 Visit friends with children the same age.
5 Use virtual communities on the internet to talk to other stay at home Dads (and stay at home Mums) to share problems, request advice, or just to have a quiet moan about things.

The first thing is to know that this is going to happen, and at least that way it is not a surprise when it does. There will be days when you end up watching the clock to see just how much of the day is left before you can get some relief from the constant childcare activity. There is always an accompanying sense of guilt with this, and a feeling of being unable to cope, but it is a perfectly normal thing to happen.

The skill is in being able to get through it. If I had my time again, one thing I would learn to do before becoming a stay at home Dad would be to meditate. I have to admit to not being in any way new age, and I have no faith in the healing power of crystals, nor have I been tempted to arrange the house on Feng Shui principles, but I do sometimes crave the ability to carry on performing mundane tasks while mentally zoning out, or to achieve moments of calm in the midst of complete chaos.

Secondly, this is where you find a way to call on your support network of other parents, family, and friends. The problems you have seem a lot less when you can get the kids to play with someone else's children while you have a cup of coffee, or when you can, even just for half an hour, leave them somewhere else being looked after by someone you trust. I know of some people who, when no family or friends are available, will use the shopping centre crèche for this exact purpose. It is inexpensive, well run, safe, and close to a coffee shop. What more could you ask?

Thirdly, the basis on which you went into being a stay at home Dad can help you through these occasional emotional crises. Most stay at home Dads made a choice to take on this role for very good reasons, other than just pragmatic financial concerns. If you can remind yourself of why you're doing this, and what you are aiming to achieve, then you can more easily convince yourself that you have to take the rough with the smooth.

If all else fails, it can be worth trying to get them to sleep. In the early months I spent a lot of time driving aimlessly round country lanes checking the rear view mirror to see if they were finally asleep.

Emotional lows are a potentially difficult area for the stay at home Dad to share completely with his partner. Whingeing after a bad day at home with the kids can reinforce every stereotype and prejudice about men's ability to effectively take care of the children, and may bring your partner the added pressure of wondering whether the right decision has been made and if you are coping effectively. In most cases, you would expect to be able to share the trials and tribulations of the day, but how this is being interpreted and whether this is creating the impression of failure is something to watch.

Finally, it is worth remembering that almost all stay at home fathers will tell you that this is the most fulfilling, rewarding and satisfying thing they have ever had the opportunity to do, and most of them consider themselves to be incredibly fortunate to have this opportunity.

Dealing with the difficult days can provide an immense feeling of satisfaction in itself. Getting a child through an illness, controlling the crying through the teething process, or working with your toddler to correct their behaviour are all tough tasks, but they are normally the ones that carry the most emotional reward.

Your Relationship

There is a view held by some that becoming a stay at home Dad may place a significant and potentially intolerable strain on a previously happy relationship. The stresses of a man constrained by a home and a woman forced to leave her children in order to make her way in the cold world every day must be too much for any relationship to bear. I have heard (at some length) about how a stay at home Dad couldn't feel as if he was man any more because he was no longer the breadwinner, and that clearly he would be immediately unattractive to his partner. The mother meanwhile will no longer have any attraction for her partner as, on her return to work, she is no longer the vision of fertile motherhood that man needs. Fortunately (for me, and for you if you're thinking about becoming a stay at home Dad) all of this would seem to be completely wrong, and the boundaries of good taste prevent me from providing you with a more fulsome description of what I think about these views.

Having been a stay at home Dad for some years now, and being in close contact with a number of stay at home Mums, many of the strains that may seem as if they would create stresses within a relationship are exactly the same for the stay at home mother. Also, the things that make a stay at home Dad's relationship successful seem to be the same as for a stay at home Mum.

A STRONG STARTING POINT

One thing that is clear is that your success as a stay at home Dad is at least in part determined by the strength of the relationship that you have with your partner. But again, this is probably true of anyone who chooses to have children, regardless of which partner is the primary carer. The sleepless nights, constant activity, mess, disruption, financial ruin, and general chaos that children bring with them seems far more likely to have an impact on a relationship than who stays home to mind the baby.

There are additional areas of potential concern as the stay at home Dad is likely to be spending the majority of his time in the company of other women, but these concerns seem to be unfounded and there are no indications of the partners of stay at home Dads being outrageously jealous of any of their 'Mum' friends. The chances are that they have met your partner and you have met theirs. Being a stay at home Dad seems to make no difference to the potential for infidelity.

STAY AT HOME DADS AND THEIR RELATIONSHIP WITH THEIR PARTNER

- Most stay at home Dads find that their role has no negative impact on their relationship with their partner. As one stay at home Dad put it, "It's not better or worse, it's just different."
- Many stay at home Dads will tell you that the role has significantly improved their relationship.
- Having one parent stay at home is seen as having brought additional stresses to the relationship; in particular this includes the financial issues of losing a salary, and the impact of children. (No surprise there.)
- However, it is also seen as significantly reducing many other stresses in

the relationship, such as lack of time at home and both partners being stressed from work.

THE CHILD EFFECT

Kids are a major change to anyone's life. They change everything from your social life ("Sorry, we couldn't get a babysitter") to your car ("For Sale, two seater hand built custom soft top. Baby forces sale".) And just about everything in between. You start reading the junk mail from life insurance companies, and worrying about schools, drugs, motorcycles, the state of the world and lots of other things. Through all of this, somehow you have to try to maintain a relationship with your partner.

There are inevitably elements of any childcare arrangement that one or both partners will not be happy with. If you have a childminder or some other form of day care provision, you are probably not happy that you aren't spending enough time with your children. The first time your child refers to the nanny as "Mummy" is probably when you decide that however good she was, she has got to go. The stay at home Dad arrangement is no different, and there are aspects of this that do cause pressures. These may include:

• Not being able to get enough time together without the children.
• Not being able to have sex (because the baby is sleeping – or not sleeping – in the bedroom with you. The baby has no idea what you're doing, but it's rare to find anyone who's comfortable with, or in fact even feels like, sex when the baby is in the room).
• Neither you nor your partner having any time completely to yourself.
• Changes to your lifestyle (in particular not being able to go out, or get away for weekends) from when you were just a couple.

- Mum not feeling she is getting enough time with the children, and certainly not enough Mum alone time with the children.

MANAGING THE CHILD EFFECT

At times it will feel as if your whole life is defined by a 'lack of': a lack of time, a lack of money and a lack of sleep.

Managing this is important to any couple. To help get over these problems it can be useful to:

- Find a babysitter or join a babysitting circle so that you can at least be sure that the lack of a babysitter is not a reason why you should be sitting at home every evening watching the baby monitor. Babysitting circles or an arrangement with one other couple to cover babysitting for each other can be a good idea as babysitters are increasingly expensive, and presumably soon will be subject to some European directive that will require you to provide them with a company car and private health insurance.
- I have found it important for both my wife and myself to be able to find time for ourselves. In my case this has entailed getting out of the house one night a week to play football, and in my wife's case by taking up some bizarre exercise classes.
- Bath and bedtime can be used as either a time when the whole family is involved in the process of getting the kids to bed, or when Mum can have some time alone with the kids, or Dad can do the bath and bedtime routine while Mum has a quiet glass of wine downstairs. It all depends on what is needed at the time.
- Given that my wife is at work all week and the evenings and weekends are the only time she gets with the kids, I try and make sure that the weekends are as protected as possible from any chores that need doing, and so are free for family time. You really don't want

to be spending your only two days together cleaning the house and ironing.

- The final piece of advice would be to keep your bed to yourselves. It seems so cute when the kids want to come and snuggle with Mum and Dad, and it is for the first few times. Just as with anything else, this sets a precedent and an expectation. If you want to sleep together alone again at any point in the next five or six years, then keep your bed to yourself, or you will have to spend all your spare cash on hotels and babysitters.

GETTING OFF ON THE RIGHT FOOT

Any potential impact on you is largely determined by the starting point, and the way in which you become a stay at home Dad. It seems that the strengths and style of the relationship you have with your partner has in fact been an enabling element for men who have become stay at home Dads. If they did not have the partner and the relationhip they had, they could not have done it in the first place. The fact that becoming a stay at home Dad did not have a negative impact on their relationship is a reflection on the relationship they already had.

However, getting the starting point right is important, and includes:

- Both partners being happy with the arrangement whereby Dad stays at home with the children. Just as it is not a good thing for the father who stays at home to be constantly wishing he were doing something else, it is also not good if your partner is spending her time wishing she didn't have to work. There is no doubt that the biggest issue faced by the partners of most stay at home fathers is the traditionally male sensation that they are missing out on their children, and this is almost inevitable. It accounts in some part for why partners of stay at home Dads are highly involved with the children on weekends and vacations. It is not about the stay at home father suddenly abrogating all responsibility just because his partner is now available for childcare duty (although let's be honest it can be a relief at times). It is about the partner wanting to be as involved as possible.

- The working mother feeling comfortable that the father will be able to cope with the childcare responsibility. This is common sense as, if the father is about to give up work while Mum returns after maternity leave, telling her employers that she is a fully committed member of staff and there are no childcare issues for them to worry about (and so stop her next promotion) it is going to be less than supportive if, three months down the line, Dad announces that he just can't do it any more. Family finances and working arrangements are thrown into complete chaos.

- The stay at home Dad avoiding any serious negative emotions about the arrangement. Complaining endlessly that you are bored, you miss your career, and that you are finding childcare dull and difficult will impose a stress on the relationship that will add to the already natural concerns of a mother returning to work.

- Ensuring that there are ground rules regarding specific sources of stress such as money and child raising style. Most stay at home Dads seem to be in relationships where disagreements on fundamental issues of childcare are the exception rather than the norm, and any problems can be resolved through discussion and compromise rather than some form of benevolent dictatorship. As a stay at home Dad you have to be continually aware of whether you are inadvertently excluding your partner from the children's development, and avoid actions that either do exclude her or appear potentially to exclude her.

- Being absolutely sure in your own mind why you are doing this, and to a certain extent also what the end game is, including how long you are planning to be a stay at home Dad, and what you are aiming to do afterwards. This helps to:

– Set the basis on which you are a stay at home Dad, ensuring your partner understands what you are doing with your time, and doesn't think you're spending your days just having fun and wasting any spare time you have. For example, if your plan is to try and return to work at some point, and you need to enhance your Information Technology skills, then doing an evening class in IT may be an integral and important part of the plan. If this isn't clear from the outset, the time and cost of an IT course may seem just to be an excuse to get out of the house and a frivolous expense.

– Provide you with some objectives to meet, other than just getting through another day without going mad. It is important, to maintain a sense of progress and personal development, to have personal objectives that you are working towards in addition to looking after the children.

• Ensuring that any discussions about plans for the day or the week are held in advance rather than in retrospect. It is always much more pleasant to discuss what you're planning to do tomorrow, rather than what on earth you did all day today.

• Finally, finding someone whom you can dump on every now and then. This may be a relative, a friend, or most likely one of the new friends you have met through the children and who can use you to dump on when required as well. This could also include sharing childcare at times by agreeing to have all the kids for a couple of hours in return for them doing the same. Sometimes, in the midst of all the chaos, all it needs is a quiet cup of coffee and the world seems a much better place.

I should mention that there are also some significant benefits to having someone at home that can help a relationship. For example you don't have to waste vacation days waiting for plumbers or home deliveries; you don't have to spend all your evenings and weekends doing shopping, cleaning, washing and ironing; you should be able to eat better as there is someone at home to make a decent dinner; and as a result you should be able to ensure that you can create spaces of time when you can be a couple, as well as when you can be a family. Well that's the theory, anyway, and there is no reason why it should not be reality in most cases.

> The most common result of being a stay at home Dad is that it doesn't make a significant difference to the relationship between him and his partner. In most cases this seems to be because of the strength and style of the relationship before they became a stay at home Dad.
>
> There is a definite need to work as a partnership, and to compromise and take into account the different stresses that each partner is dealing with, but by working as a partnership and managing time to the best effect, it is possible to maintain your relationship, enjoy being a family, and still enjoy being a couple as well.

Living in a Woman's World

It would be nice to think that it doesn't matter whether it is Mum or Dad who stays at home to look after the children, and that the world exists equally for men and for women. It would also be nice to think that you can just as easily integrate into the world of stay at home parenthood as a man as you can as a woman, but however much similarity there is in the issues you face, you have to realise that as soon as you become a stay at home father you are leaving behind the normality you once knew and entering a whole new world.

A STRANGE NEW WORLD

This new world is, without any doubt at all, fundamentally a woman's world. It is different from the world you knew and at times it can be frightening, frustrating, confusing and even downright unpleasant. It can also be interesting, enlightening, reassuring, and very, very funny, particularly when the subject of men comes up in the conversation.

Every day there is something that will remind you that you are in a world that is designed for women and focused on women and their needs. While in some ways this is understandable, there are times when it can get to be annoying. The first time I noticed that the world was slightly different was when I found myself in the town centre on a weekday morning. It was one of those odd occasions when I could tell that something was different, but I couldn't quite put my finger on what it was. After about an hour it dawned on me. I hardly ever went into town on weekdays before I became a stay at home Dad. It was always the weekend. During the week I noticed that there were no men. At least there were no men under 60. There were none at all, or at least none that you could notice. Everyone in town seemed to be female and with a pushchair.

I had a sudden realisation that while men were at work thinking that they were running the world, there was in fact either a parallel universe in which we were fundamentally irrelevant, or that while we were safely chained to our desks, the real world was carrying on without us, and was completely dominated by women. I have learned that it is best not to make any judgement as to whether this is a good thing or not.

BEING THE ONLY MAN

As you get out and about with your children, and quite probably start to attend some kind of toddler group or organised entertainment sessions with the kids, as a stay at home Dad you have to get used to being the only man in a room full of young mothers. This really is nothing like any teenage fantasy you may have, and some stay at home Dads find this situation quite intimidating.

There can be a definite sensation that you are somehow intruding on some private function to which you weren't invited, and this can be offputting at first.

This whole process of attending functions where you are the only man is greatly improved if you already know someone who is attending, and this is one area where having met some mothers through the whole antenatal process is a great help. At least there is one friendly face there that will smile at you across the room. This at least prevents any feelings of complete social isolation, and can provide a link to the rest of the group.

Integration into these groups does, in my experience, tend to be a short term problem, but it always seems to be up to the stay at home Dad to make the effort to break the ice in some way. It is naturally easier for new mothers to talk to one another than it is to start a conversation with the only man in the room. Your contribution to the subjects of childbirth, sore nipples, and breastfeeding techniques are likely to be minimal, as well as significantly less amusing than you thought.

Interestingly, many young mothers find the process of breaking into these toddler groups as daunting as a stay at home Dad, so although at first sight it may seem as if there is some kind of gender bias going on, it is probably less than you think, and may be more a reflection of the gender paranoia that some stay at home Dads initially suffer from.

SUBTLE DISCRIMINATION

There are more subtle ways in which living in a woman's world strikes you on a regular basis. Public lavatories, while not high on everyone's list of things that are important to them, assume a bizarre significance in your life once you are out and about with small children. Although there is an increasing number of parent and child facilities provided, where these are not available almost invariably any child friendly facilities have been added to the ladies lavatory while the men's toilets seem to remain a nineteenth century construction of cracked urinals and broken toilet seats.

Even where there are parent and child facilities, as a stay at home Dad you have to get used to being an unwelcome interruption to a mother who thought she would be able to breastfeed in a private setting. Once again you can get the impression that you are an intruder: on one occasion when I used one of these facilities to change a nappy I was asked by a woman I had never seen before if I would like to wait outside while she changed it for me. Tempting as the offer was, pride overcame any desire to avoid my unpleasant duty and I graciously declined the offer much to her bemusement.

The suggestion that I should be incapable of changing a nappy is an indication of a wider feeling that many stay at home Dads experience, which is that there is a general impression that somehow we're just not quite up to the job. While we may lack some of the essential biology for childbirth and breastfeeding, there are days when the condescending and patronising reactions can be intensely irritating. At times this is even meant well as mothers comment that "you're so good with the children." The unspoken addition "for a man" is always there. Most stay at home Dads report this experience in some form, even from health professionals, and their own family. My experience is that there is nothing you can do about this. If you want to fight a battle against thousands of years of gender stereotyping then carry on, but generally I have more important things to do – like the washing and the cleaning.

At times though there are moments that I find genuinely touching. As a rule women are much more considerate to anyone with a pushchair or pram, and despite chivalrous tendencies I am only too willing to let anyone hold a shop door open for me, or hold the bottom of the pushchair to help get it down a flight of stairs. Your masculine pride would feel remarkably stupid as you and your child tumble gracelessly down the steps.

The final area where the stay at home Dad has to be able to recognise that he is no longer in a man's world is when you read anything connected with the subject of childcare. Almost without exception any parenting magazines or childcare texts assume that Dad is at work and that it is Mum who has stayed at home to look after the children. The majority of them seem to assume that Dad has no idea what to do with a child, and is most likely in the pub or playing football.[8]

This isn't really surprising, as there is a much larger population of stay at home mothers than there is of stay at home fathers, but the stereotype can start to grate fairly quickly. The unfortunate thing is that you do have to put up with this, as there is an immense amount of useful information in some of these books, as long as you are able to translate it.

ADAPT AND SURVIVE

You have to adapt to survive in this new world, and it is useful to understand that you are unlikely to have many in-depth conversations concerning anything of an even vaguely male nature for some time. Most of the conversation is connected to children, which is fine because you have at least one of those and can bore for your country on the subject. It is also inevitable that after a while you will become increasingly comfortable in your role as a stay at home Dad and your place in a woman's world, although when I found myself clipping recipes from my wife's magazines I realised that it was possible to get too comfortable.

There is a certain amount of pride to be had from adapting to this world and in doing your best to integrate and participate fully in it. It is not long before the magazines your partner buys do actually start to look more interesting than the ones you insist on buying. Recipes, how to get stains out of the carpet, and price comparisons on new

8 Apart from White Ladder books – Ed.

vacuum cleaners are all subjects with which you now need to be intimately familiar. It will at least give you something to contribute at the next coffee morning.

TIPS FOR DEALING WITH BEING THE ONLY MAN IN THE ROOM

- Smile and be approachable.
- Make it clear that you are there with your children.
- Do not comfort a crying child who is with someone you don't know, or have not made some form of contact with. The potential for this to be misinterpreted is (sadly) too high.
- Don't make a big deal about being the only man. The more normal you make it seem, the more normal it will be.
- Persevere and don't be put off by initial suspicion.
- Don't let one unfriendly mother put you off the whole group.
- Don't try and join in the breastfeeding conversations. Find a subject where you can make a contribution.

Living in a woman's world does also mean that the stay at home Dad has, for the majority of his time, left behind the man's world that he was once a part of, and obviously there are elements of this that any man would miss. This is why many stay at home Dads report the need to go off and do something manly as a form of relief from their childcare role.

Leaving behind the man's world can also introduce some concerns for stay at home Dads regarding how they will be perceived in the long term. While there is no evidence to suggest that children who are part of a stay at home Dad household suffer in any way when compared to those where the mother stayed at home, or both parents work, you do start to worry about how your children will feel when they are asked what their father does, or what you are going to do when there is a 'take your child to work day'. While additional help with the household chores may be useful, you have to imagine that this probably wasn't what they had in mind.

The Long Term

It really doesn't seem long before the newborn child you held in your arms is waving a tearful goodbye at the school gates and asking you if it would be possible for you to pick them up around the corner from school because it isn't cool to have Dad waiting for them at three o'clock. Actually, a lot of the days do seem long, but the weeks, months and years seem to fly by.

Although childcare responsibilities don't end when they get to be five (or even 35 I am told) it is most likely that once they are at school, the majority of stay at home fathers will be looking for something productive to do during term time between the hours of 9.00 and 3.00. Most stay at home fathers aim to return to work as soon as practical, not only for something to do, but also for pragmatic financial reasons.

STAY AT HOME FATHERS' PLANS WHEN THE KIDS GO TO SCHOOL

- Many stay at home Dads do not expect to retain the primary carer role once the children go to school. Of these the majority expect the care for the children to be equally shared between them and their partner.
- The majority of stay at home fathers expect to return to work full time in the future.
- Most stay at home fathers do not have a definite plan to return to a specific job. Some expect to use the break in their working lives to

completely change their career direction. There is no assumption that they will return to their previous line of employment.

• Where stay at home fathers have career breaks from their employer, they expect to return to that employer after the career break. (This seems to be a rare situation however.)

Although most stay at home Dads aim to return to employment, the childcare issues do not go away once the kids are at school. In particular there are the school holidays, the short school day, and the inevitable childhood illnesses and school absences that have to be considered. These all have an impact on the type of role that the stay at home Dad can consider for his return to productive society, and also on the role and responsibilities of the working mother.

PLANNING FOR RETURNING TO WORK

Ideally, when starting out as a stay at home father you had a plan for when the childcare responsibilities reduced, or at least some idea of what you wanted to do in the long term. With this plan in mind, during the childcare years you have been working diligently towards that plan in some way. It may have been retraining, or acquiring new skills; it may have been developing an idea for your own business or it may be some creative enterprise, but you have had five plus years in which to get ready to implement your long term plan.

Alternatively, it may be that the point when the children go to school is the first time at which you can start to work towards that plan by attending training courses or putting the time into your own enterprise. Either way, the thing you really don't want to be doing at this point is watching daytime television. (Unless of course you have embarked on a career as a commentator on popular culture as a day-time television critic.)

WHAT STAY AT HOME DADS DO TO PREPARE FOR THE RETURN TO WORK

Stay at home Dads have taken a variety of approaches to maintaining their skills or contacts in preparation for a return to work or the development of a new career. Many have found this difficult particularly when the children are young, and any real preparation for returning to work has been planned around when funded daycare places become available. As well as developing and maintaining skills, some of this activity has been specifically focused on avoiding a five year blank gap in the CV when it becomes time to look for work.

1 Formal retraining for a new career, particularly one that will enable them to combine childcare responsibilities for children at school with their career.
2 Self study for new skills, in particular IT.
3 Maintaining contact with ex-colleagues.
4 Continuing to read industry publications and conduct Internet based research.
5 Working on an occasional basis as a self-employed consultant.
6 Becoming involved in voluntary work.

In terms of what you will be able to do, it is worth knowing in advance that it is very likely that your experiences as a stay at home father will have changed you as a person. It may well have changed your attitude towards work and redefined your priorities in such a way that traditional corporate success is no longer your prime objective.

You are likely to be more home oriented, and more focused on being able to continue to spend time with the children and the family. By being a stay at home father you will almost certainly have expanded your own horizons, and extended the range of possibilities that are open to you – or that you are open to – for your future career. Becoming a stay at home father was a major change, and undoubtedly takes a lot of courage, whether you know it at the time or not. Opportunities that may have been daunting before you became a stay at home father may now look decidedly more achievable, from making a career out of doing up properties to fulfilling a dream to become a writer or artist. Once you have been a full time father nothing seems impossible any more.

It is also likely that in many cases you will both need and want to structure your working life around a continuing role as the primary carer for the children. Given that you have spent the last five or more years focusing on the development of your partner's career, earnings and pension, putting her career second to yours and the children is probably not a sensible financial decision.

 Since it is likely that the initial decision to become a stay at home father was probably at least in part based on the relative earning power of you and your partner, it is unlikely that after a five year career break your earnings will suddenly exceed your partner's. Some stay at home fathers find that they want to continue in their role as the primary carer, and work remains a definite second priority.

YOU'RE NOT THE PERSON YOU USED TO BE

My time as a stay at home Dad has been a life changing experience that has helped to put a lot of things into what I would now consider to be their proper perspective. It has been the most important and enjoyable thing that I have ever done, and I find it hard to believe that I ever spent 10 hours a day in the office, and that I was misguided enough ever to believe that what I was doing was even vaguely important. As I result, I have absolutely no doubt that I will never be able to return to the same kind of career I had before becoming a stay at home Dad.

I suspect I have been permanently ruined for the world of work. I just wouldn't be able to take enough of the daily issues seriously, and I certainly wouldn't be able to let it get in the way of looking after the kids and being there for every important occasion. In a way this is unfortunate, as being a stay at home Dad has certainly given me skills and personal attributes that would make me a better member of any workforce. For example:

- I am now more patient with people.
- I am better able to multi-task and prioritise activities.
- I am better at explaining tasks, setting objectives, and understanding problems encountered in achieving those objectives.
- I am more able to bring a sense of perspective to any crisis or major issue.
- I am able to continue with tasks long past the point at which total mental and physical exhaustion has been reached.

With the above attributes I suspect I would make a great employee as long as any prospective employer could put up with the fact that I would view almost any job similar to those I have done before as a trivial and meaningless activity compared with being a stay at home father.

HOW BEING A STAY AT HOME DAD HAS CHANGED THOSE WHO DO IT

Almost all stay at home Dads will tell you that their time as stay at home father has changed them in many ways. Specific changes include:

Have become more:

- Calm
- Patient
- Tolerant
- Focused on what is really important
- Focused on the family unit
- Assertive
- Self-motivated
- Able to adapt to situations
- Able to deal with change
- Sociable
- Understanding of women
- Optimistic
- Appreciative of partner
- Self-aware

Have become less:

- Stressed
- Selfish
- Competitive
- Materialistic and acquisitive

Overall, most stay at home Dads seem to believe that the role has improved them as a person.

Many of the changes that stay at home Dads will cite may be an inevitable effect of fatherhood regardless of whether Dad is the one to stay at home or not, but many of them also come about as a result of the rigours of daily childcare responsibilities. For example, assertiveness is essential and almost natural, not only when dealing with an errant toddler, but also when being given a pat answer by medical professionals or teachers. There is no doubt in my mind that time as a stay at home Dad makes it almost impossible not to become a more rounded individual.

There is a final important point to consider when planning a return to work, and that is to have a very clear plan as to what you can say at an interview to explain your absence from the workforce for the last five or more years.

Most mothers find it difficult to re-enter the workplace after a five year plus break to raise children to school age, and then face the challenges of a work environment that is not parent friendly. In most cases, this results in being five years or more behind the career path they had expected, and seeing younger and less capable people being promoted ahead of them.

The same issues will face the stay at home Dad. It is just as well that we have become more focused on our families and less competitive and materialistic. If we hadn't then returning to work was probably going to be an intensely depressing experience.

In the long term most stay at home Dads will return to work in some form. Most have no clear plan for what type of work they intend to do, and many are planning to use this career break to change direction. For many men, a childcare role seems to present a real opportunity to break away from their existing career and try something new; something that can potentially include an element of childcare as well as a job.

However, it does seem to be important to have a plan for preparing yourself for any new opportunity by using your time away from the workplace to develop the skills and acquire experience that may help you when you want to undertake something more permanent. By having a long term plan you can help to allay concerns that friends and family may have about your role as a stay at home Dad and you can be prepared for the day when you wave goodbye at the school gates and the rest of the day is your own.

CONCLUSION

Becoming a Stay at Home Dad

Despite all the potential long term difficulties, and all the issues and challenges associated with being a stay at home Dad, it is difficult to find any stay at home father who says he has any real regrets about it. Almost without exception they will tell you that if you think you want to be a stay at home Dad then take the leap. You will never know how good it is until you do it.

ADVICE FROM STAY AT HOME DADS FOR THOSE THINKING ABOUT IT

Do

- Plan for your role as a stay at home Dad.
- Be flexible.
- Be open minded.
- Build a support network.
- Get fit before you start.
- Make sure it is what you really want to do.
- Have a trial run if possible before the final decision has to be made about which partner will go back to work.
- Be prepared to adapt.
- Get out of the house every day.
- Remember you're not alone.

Don't

- Expect to be able to stick to the plan you have made.
- Ignore the fact that your partner is making sacrifices by going to work.
- Assume you will have lots of free time.
- Expect children to fit in with you. It's the other way round most of the time.
- Take any notice of the mothers with attitude.
- Expect it to be easy.

Being a stay at home Dad is one of those strange things that you may well start off doing just for the usual pragmatic and highly sensible financial reasons, but you only keep doing because it is a great thing to do. It may well be the most important thing you ever do in your life, it provides laughter and fun every day, and although it's impossible to describe why you're doing it, every day that you spend with your kids, you know exactly why, and you know that it's an experience that you are privileged to have the opportunity to enjoy.

There are difficulties for both Mum and Dad when Dad stays at home, but these are not insurmountable, and the arrangement can be the best for all concerned. What matters most is whether the arrangement is the best for the children. Happy and fulfilled parents go a long way to creating the right environment for happy children as well. If being a stay at home Dad will do this for you, and being a working Mum will do it for your partner, then ignore what anyone says to you, write a plan, be prepared to throw it away, and make sure you can tell which appliance is the washing machine.

APPENDIX

Useful Websites

There is a huge amount of general parenting information available on the Internet. While the websites below do not represent an exhaustive list, they do include some that you may find useful as a stay at home Dad.

www.homedad.org.uk
The homedad site is dedicated to stay at home Dads. It offers discussion boards, a chat room, and useful information.

www.fathersdirect.com
This site is aimed at all fathers, not just stay at home Dads, but it does look specifically at issues of fatherhood and contains a range of research material and useful information.

www.nct.org.uk
Website of the National Childbirth Trust.

www.fq-magazine.com
Website for the father's magazine FQ.

www.dwp.gov.uk
The Department of Work and Pensions, for all that vital information about pensions.

www.dfee.gov.uk
Anything and everything concerning education.

www.ofsted.gov.uk

Inspection reports for schools and other useful information.

www.forparentsbyparents.com

Lots of parenting information from parents.

CONTACT US

You're welcome to contact White Ladder Press if you have any questions or comments for either us or the author. Please use whichever of the following routes suits you.

Phone: 01803 813343 between 9am and 5.30pm

Email: enquiries@whiteladderpress.com

Fax: 01803 813928

Address: White Ladder Press, Great Ambrook, Near Ipplepen, Devon TQ12 5UL

Website: www.whiteladderpress.com

COULD YOU BE A BARKER?

No, we're not casting aspersions on your character. We mean Barker in the sense of town crier or advocate. Our White Ladder Barkers spread the word and build themselves a business (part time or full time is up to you) while they do it.

We're always keen to find enthusiastic and motivated people who want to earn some money – or fundraise for a local school or favourite charity – by selling our books. The deal's very simple. We provide the books at a healthy discount, and you sell them on at full price and keep the difference. There's a modest minimum order. You can sell on an ongoing basis, on stalls at events such as school fairs, coffee mornings or business get-togethers, and you can organise events and parties to sell the books.

Our books are fun, quirky and genuinely useful, and many of your customers will have seen the extensive press coverage the books get. So they're easy to sell and, because they're fun (and often funny), they're a great talking point with friends and customers.

Once you decide you like the idea of being a Barker, call Richard on 01803 814124 and he'll sort you out with your first consignment of books. We'd love you to join us.

Recipes *for* Disaster*s*

How to turn kitchen cock-ups
into magnificent meals

"Methinks 'twould have spared me much grief had I had this cunning volume to hand when I burnt those cursèd cakes." *King Alfred the Great*

It was all going so well... friends for lunch, guests for dinner, family for Christmas. You're planning a delicious meal, relaxed yet sophisticated, over which everyone can chat, drink a glass of fine wine and congratulate you on your culinary talent.

And then, just as you were starting to enjoy it – disaster! The pastry has burnt, the pudding has collapsed or the terrine won't turn out. Or the main ingredient has been eaten by the cat. Or perhaps it's the guests who've buggered everything up: they forgot to mention that they're vegetarian (you've made a beef bourguignon). Or they've brought along a friend (you've only made six crème brûlées).

But don't panic. There are few kitchen cock-ups that can't be successfully salvaged if you know how. With the right attitude you are no longer accident-prone, but adaptable. Not a panicker but a creative, inspirational cook. Recipes for Disasters is packed with useful tips and ideas for making sure that your entertaining always runs smoothly (or at least appears to, whatever is going on behind the scenes). Yes, you still can have a reputation as a culinary paragon, even if it is all bluff.

OUT OF YOUR TOWNIE MIND

THE REALITY BEHIND THE DREAM OF COUNTRY LIVING

"Richard Craze yanks the rose-tinted spectacles from the rural idyll and tramples them in the mud. The result is cheeky but charming — a kind of Feel-the-Fear-But-Do-It-Anyway for wannabe downshifters." **Hugh Fearnley-Whittingstall**

We all have our own fantasy of what life in the country will be like. But are we right? Is it all roses round the door, or are they really brambles?

So you're finally sick of city life. You close your eyes and dream of living in the country – all that space, and wonderful views. Going for long walks and coming home to an open fire, bringing your children up healthy and safe and being part of a community. Maybe you have visions of baking cakes on an Aga, keeping your own hens and handknitting your own yoghurt...

But will it really be like that?

Out of Your Townie Mind takes the most popular dreams of rural life that townies have (based on a survey of aspiring country dwellers) and lays the real facts on the line. Does a big garden really give you more space to enjoy the country, or just create so much work you never have time to enjoy it? Will a house in the woods be a private haven of wildlife, your own nature reserve on the doorstep... or is it just dark, damp and a recipe for endless gutter clearing?

Out of Your Townie Mind **shows you how, with a bit of forethought, you can get the very best out of country living by avoiding the pitfalls other townies stumble into.**

KIDS&Co

"Ros Jay has had a brilliant idea, and what is more she has executed it brilliantly. **KIDS & CO** is the essential handbook for any manager about to commit the act of parenthood, and a thoroughly entertaining read for everyone else"
JOHN CLEESE

WHEN IT COMES TO RAISING YOUR KIDS, YOU KNOW MORE THAN YOU THINK.

So you spent five or ten years working before you started your family? Maybe more? Well, don't waste those hard-learned skills. Use them on your kids. Treat your children like customers, like employees, like colleagues.

No, really.

Just because you're a parent, your business skills don't have to go out of the window when you walk in throughthe front door. You may sometimes feel that the kids get the better of you every time, but here's one weapon you have that they don't: all those business skills you already have and they know nothing about. Closing the sale, win/win negotiating, motivational skills and all the rest.

Ros Jay is a professsional author who writes on both business and parenting topics, in this case simultaneously. She is the mother of three young children and stepmother to another three grown-up ones.

THE VOICE OF TOBACCO

"An amazing new book on smoking — it has great style and humour, and is brilliantly funny. Read this happy smoker's guide — if only I had been the author."
LESLIE PHILLIPS

What does the Voice of Tobacco say to you?
There's no need to give up; just cutting down will do.
How can it be bad for you when it feels so good?
Just one cigarette can't hurt you, now can it?

It's hard not to listen. Especially when, from the other side of the debate, we smokers have all been lectured by self-righteous prigs who think that (a) we should want to give up and (b) giving up smoking should be easy.

Well we don't and it ain't.

And yet there does come a time when, no matter how much we enjoy smoking, we have to become not smokers.

Richard Craze's guide gives it to you straight: what it's really like to give up smoking. The headaches, the sleeplessness, the irritability. And The Voice. He's been there and his diary reports back from the front line. It may not be pleasant, but it's honest. It may or may not help you to give up smoking, but it will certainly get you looking at smoking in a new way. And it will give you something to do with your hands.

This is the diary of a dedicated and happy smoker who is now not smoking. Here's how he did it. Here's how to do it without the trauma, the withdrawal symptoms, the twitching, the bad temper. Yeah, right. In your dreams.

The
White
Ladder
Diaries

"To start a business from scratch with a great idea but little money is a terrifying but thrilling challenge. White Ladder is a fine example of how sheer guts and drive can win the day."
TIM WATERSTONE

Have you ever dreamed of starting your own business?

Want to know what it's like? I mean, what it's really like?

Ros Jay and her partner, Richard Craze, first had the idea for White Ladder Press in the summer of 2002. This is the story of how they overcame their doubts and anxieties and brought the company to life, for only a few thousand pounds, and set it on its way to being a successful publishing company (this is its third book).

The White Ladder Diaries isn't all theory and recollections. It's a real life, day-by-day diary of all those crucial steps, naïve mistakes and emotional moments between conceiving the idea for a business and launching the first product. It records the thinking behind all the vital decisions, from choosing a logo or building a website, to sorting out a phone system or getting to grips with discounts.

What's more, the diary is littered with tips and advice for anyone else starting up a business. Whether you want to know how to register a domain name or how to write a press release, it's all in here.

If they could do it, so can you. Go on – stop dreaming.
Be your own boss.

Babies

for Beginners

If it isn't in here, you don't need to know it.

At last, here is the book for every new parent who's never been quite sure what a cradle cap is and whether you need one. **Babies for Beginners** cuts the crap — the unnecessary equipment, the overfussy advice — and gives you the absolute basics of babycare: keep the baby alive, at all costs, and try to stop it getting too hungry.

From bedtime to bathtime, mealtime to playtime, this book highlights the CORE OBJECTIVE of each exercise (for example, get the baby bathed) and the KEY FOCUS (don't drown it). By exploding the myths around each aspect of babycare, the book explains what is necessary and what is a bonus; what equipment is essential and what you can do without.

Babies for Beginners is the perfect book for every first time mother who's confused by all the advice and can't believe it's really necessary to spend that much money. And it's the ultimate guide for every father looking for an excuse to get out of ante-natal classes.

Roni Jay is a professional author whose books include **KIDS & Co: winning business tactics for every family.** She is the mother of three young children, and stepmother to another three grown up ones.

ORDER FORM

You can order any of our books via any of the contact routes on page 114, including on our website. Or fill out the order form below and fax it or post it to us.

We'll normally send your copy out by first class post within 24 hours (but please allow five days for delivery). We don't charge postage and packing within the UK. Please add £1 per book for postage outside the UK.

Title (Mr/Mrs/Miss/Ms/Dr/Lord etc)

Name

Address

Postcode

Daytime phone number

Email

No. of copies	Title	Price	Total £
	Full Time Father	£9.99	
	Recipes for Disasters	£7.99	
	Out of Your Townie Mind	£7.99	
	Kids & Co	£6.99	
	Babies for Beginners	£6.99	
	The White Ladder Diaries	£9.99	
	The Voice of Tobacco	£6.99	
	Postage and packing £1 per book (outside the UK only):		
	TOTAL:		

Please either send us a cheque made out to White Ladder Press Ltd or fill in the credit card details below.

Type of card ☐ Visa ☐ Mastercard ☐ Switch

Card number

Start date (if on card) _____ Expiry date _____ Issue no (Switch) _____

Name as shown on card

Signature